Teaching the
Universe
of Discourse

Teaching the Universe of Discourse

JAMES MOFFETT

BOYNTON/COOK PUBLISHERS
HEINEMANN
PORTSMOUTH, NH

Boynton/Cook Publishers
A subsidiary of Reed Elsevier Inc.
361 Hanover Street, Portsmouth, NH 03801-3912
Offices and agents throughout the world

Library of Congress Cataloging-in-Publication Data

Moffett, James.
    Teaching the universe of discourse/James Moffett.
      p.   cm.
    Reprint. Originally published: Boston: Houghton Mifflin, 1983.
    Includes bibliographical references.
    ISBN 0-86709-181-9
    1. Language arts. 2. English language—Composition and exercises.
I. Title.
LB1576.M573 1987   87-27816
808'.042'07—dc19   CIP

Printed in the United States of America
  94 95 96 97   10 9 8 7

FOREWORD TO 1983 REISSUE

THE PURPOSE of a reissue is to continue to make available a book that has won an enduring berth with its readership. It is not a revision, and so changes do not appear. One has to have faith that the book holds as is. Although I feel some pangs at references that could be updated, and I regret the unintentionally sexist prevalence of *he,* I can definitely say that I still stand behind the ideas.

It is in the nature of theory that it should not obsolesce as rapidly as information or more concrete exposition, but it also exists as an hypothesis to be modified, as a think-piece. The question is whether the modification should take place in the original book or in the minds of the readers. The practical experience and formal research that could corroborate or invalidate the theory developed in this book accumulate slowly, and the central thesis that stages of discourse correspond to levels of abstraction (if "abstraction" is specially defined) may never be susceptible of ultimate proof, like many other comprehensive theories about human functioning. But as I said within, I am after a strategic gain in concept: you are advised not so much to believe these ideas as to utilize them.

In those areas where I did cite research more than casually — developmental psychology and syntactic growth — new work has of course been done but none that vitiates the ideas. In fact, some rather direct testing of the developmental hypothesis in both the United States and the United Kingdom has tended to bear it out. James Britton has written of England's Writing Research Unit, "What does come through . . . (from a limited sample of about two thousand scripts, the work of 500 boys and girls in 65 schools) is the firm nature of the association between Moffett's abstractive scale and progress through the years of schooling."[1] And the sort of argument I raised against formal sentence-combining must still be reckoned with now that the latest such exercises have tried to meet its objections. Combining given sentences into a "whole discourse" does not keep these new exercises from being arhetorical, since they still do not engage the student in authentic *composing*. Further, the experiments that claim to show that such exercises improve the sentences that come out in actual composing neither measure for negative side-effects nor compare this "progress" with what would have been achieved had students spent the same amount of time doing real authoring in workshop groups taught to combine sentences as an organic part of revising papers together (the alternative recommended herein). In any case, research in these areas goes on at such a pace that updating for a book is futile; it is a task for journals.

Just as the ideas in this book must be thrown up continually against current evidence — not least of all the direct experience from the classroom — so must the theory be extended and amended by readers for themselves. More than anything else, I meant for readers to undergo certain thinking experiences that would later help them to conceive more usefully their educational mission. For this reason, it is not pertinent for me to revise the theory to overcome shortcomings or to incorporate others' modifications. One can read elsewhere how others have amended or applied it. Though I may not agree with some of these revisions, I recognize that the book's main value may be less to convince than to stimulate. This is consistent with my originally having sketched the theory suggestively rather than having systematically filled it in.

A few readers have felt that the book does not deal enough with literature, especially poetry. I was acutely aware when writing it that most English teachers know *only* literature, because college English majors study little else as their speciality.

---

[1] James Britton, "Language and the Nature of Learning," in *The Teaching of English: The 76th Yearbook of the National Society for the Study of Education,* ed. James Squire (Chicago: University of Chicago Press, 1977), p. 34.

Though my own background was chiefly literary — and treating poetry more would have been a luxury for me — I felt that where teachers failed they did so from imperception about how learning occurs, about the *processes* of making and interpreting symbols, the inner workings behind the talking, reading, and writing. Too many teachers were thrilled by literature but chilled by youngsters, because they had nowhere acquired understanding of what learning to discourse entails for human beings. So I set out to build a bridge, intellectually rigorous but emotionally true also, between the familiar world of literature, books, and talk and the discursive universe of the mind that these manifest. I based the structure of English on the primal communication triad, which permits relating literature to life, language forms to modes of thought. I wanted to recast into the psychological terms of human growth those familiar but opaque academic elements such as rhetoric, logic, grammar, and literary technique, because I felt obliged to help teachers where they needed help most.

However warranted this approach may have been, I unwittingly threw off some readers who did not recognize just how much in fact I was dealing with literature or how dear it was to me, so different did it appear to them in the greatly expanded context of the *total* universe of discourse. In a long chapter devoted to drama and another to fiction I focused on the real-life counterparts and the developmental significance of various dramaturgical and fictional techniques. To poetry I allotted a whole dimension running the entire length of the abstractive scale. By spreading it across the varieties of drama, description, narrative, and reflection I hoped to open up classroom possibilities for it. But I did not, it is true, trace out myself all these possibilities, trusting teachers rather to draw on the college training they *did* have. But perhaps I should have indulged myself more.

The further specifying and applying of ideas in this book is precisely the business of *Student-Centered Language Arts and Reading, K-13: A Handbook for Teachers* (the title of the newer editions of *A Student-Centered Language Arts Curriculum*). It

INTRODUCTION

MOST CHILDREN, by the time they are ready to begin school, know the full contents of an introductory text in transformational grammar. One such text is a bit more than 400 pages long and it covers declaratives and interrogatives, affirmatives and negatives, actives and passives, simple sentences, conjoined sentences and some kinds of embedded sentences. The preschool child knows all this. Not explicitly, of course. He has not formulated his grammatical knowledge and he cannot talk about it in transformational or any other terms. His knowledge is implicit, implicit in the range of sentences he understands and in the range he is able to construct. He operates *as if* he possessed the structural knowledge which is *formally represented* by a transformational grammar. Which is not to say that he knows anything of the representation itself or would even be capable of learning it.

The Russian children's poet, Kornei Chukovsky, calls the preschool child, any preschool child, "a linguistic genius" and the accolade is deserved if we think only of the acquisition of grammar. However, the child is an uneven genius. If we set him a task of communication, even a very elementary one, the genius gives way to the child. The quality of a communication can only be judged against a criterion, something which the communication can be seen to have accomplished or failed to accomplish. Let us consider a simple problem which is of this kind, a problem that has been set to preschool children. Two children are involved: a speaker, or encoder, and a receiver, or decoder. They sit on opposite sides of a table with an opaque screen between them. Each child has the same four pictures in front of him: a dog standing up; a dog lying down; a cat standing up; a cat lying down. The encoder picks out any one he likes and the experimenter directs him to describe it so that his interlocutor on the other side of the screen can identify the one intended. The elements of discourse are all here: speaker, listener, and topic. In terms of James Moffett's "levels of abstraction" the problem is extremely concrete.

The preschool child and even the child in the early school years proves to have no great genius for discourse. As speaker, for example, his performance is likely to show the following sorts of defects:

1. Difficulty relying exclusively on language. He wants to point and the experimenter has to insist that this is a "no hands" task and perhaps ask him to put his hands behind his back. Even then the fingers twitch to help out the tongue.

2. Egocentrism. He is likely to use terms and draw upon experiences that his interlocutor does not share — perhaps calling one of the dogs "Jip" because it reminds him of his cousin's dog "Jip." He is egocentric in the sense that he fails to take account of the discrepancy between his own informational position and that of his auditor. Mr. Moffett shows in this book how profound and long lasting a problem egocentrism is in communication.

3. Failure to analyze the given information according to the problem. He is likely not to realize that the names of the animal and of its posture together serve uniquely to characterize each picture. Indeed, in describing one picture a child may look only at that one, ignoring the contrast array, and so say a great many things about the picture which have no utility at all for the task: "It's a dog and it has a spot on its back and one leg is crooked and you can see its whiskers," etc.

The minimal discourse situation described above exposes certain fundamental deficiencies of performance, but there are many others, applying to young children, older children, even adults, which can be exposed only if more complex problems are assigned. Suppose the child or adult is asked to give directions for finding someone's house or to tell a story he has heard or to improvise dialogue in a play or to explain something he has learned and understood in history or in physics. Will he be able to order information so that the listener knows what he needs to know at each point in an exposition? Will his embedded sentences convey appropriate figure–ground relations by subordinating linguistically that which is subordinate psychologically? Will his conjoinings be logical or will they only concatenate? Does he use his transformations just where they are appropriate, producing a sequence of constructions that describes a line of thought? Can he maintain a consistent point of view when he wants to and change when he wants to do that? Can he shift styles to suit different sorts of decoders? Can he find a metaphor that captures the essentials of an entire intellectual structure? None of these skills is entailed in grammatical knowledge. None of them is well developed in early childhood. None of them can be said to have a definable ceiling but most of us get nowhere near the ceiling that the best writers and speakers make visible to us.

By what means can communication skills be taught? I agree with Mr. Moffett that it is extremely improbable that they should be affected at all by instruction in explicit grammar, whether that grammar be traditional or transformational circa 1958, or transformational circa 1965, or on the current transformational frontier. Study of the theory of the language is probably completely irrelevant to the development of skill in the use of the language. Of course the theory may have interest or value in its own right. "Proving" sentences with grammatical axioms has something of the fascination of geometry. "Now all we need," someone has said, "is a good argument for the study of geometry."

I agree again with the author that skills are not likely to be taught by dicta concerning the value of particular constructions, lexical items, or marks of punctuation, nor by drills in the use of them. A student is likely to learn something more absolute than the teacher intends; perhaps that complex sentences are better than simple sentences or that *do not* is preferable to *don't* or that the semicolon is an elegant mark of punctuation. An alert student who discovers that his teacher has a fondness for the semicolon will cheerfully strew semicolons in that teacher's path. What the students needs, of course, is a rich set of options and a sense of how to employ them rather than a notion that any particular option is uncontingently admirable.

Surely skills are acquired by practice and so it is a step forward to ask students to write themes as most teachers do. But practice without unequivocal, well timed, valued, and properly representative feedback will not work and that is the problem with much theme writing. As Mr. Moffett says, the student who writes or speaks to only one addressee, the same old teacher, cannot very well learn how to communicate in the range of situations that life presents. If the feedback he receives, in the form of marginal comments, is thoughtful it is likely to be long delayed and the student will have lost interest in, or quite forgotten, what it was he intended to convey. If the feedback is more promptly delivered it is likely to be more superficially based, nearer the proofreading level — a response to the surface of his message which does not tell him whether the message itself was or was not received.

In a conversation I have remembered for a long time, a teacher of English in high school, having reviewed his instructional repertoire of sentence parsing, theme grading, and teaching the parts of speech, sighed and said: "There must be something better than this." With the publication of James Moffett's book I feel able to say: "There is."

Mr. Moffett would teach the Universe of Discourse not by analyzing language but by having students use it in every realistic way. Languages are not content subjects, like history or physics; they are symbol systems and the great thing to learn about symbol systems is how to manipulate them, not how to analyze them. Symbol manipulation is to be learned by engaging in discourse of all kinds, the sequence recapitulating the levels of abstraction that seem to characterize intellectual growth.

Mr. Moffett would build the young student's repertoire of conjoinings and embeddings by a kind of expanding dialogue in which the student sets the topic with an initial sentence and the instructor encourages elaboration with questions and qualifications and emendations. He would have students become conscious of levels of abstraction in association with the relations of discourse by having them write, as well as read, interior monologues, private diaries, personal letters, autobiography, biography, history, and science. He would have students discover the problems of dramatic dialogue by having them, for example, improvise the scene in which Cassius works upon Brutus before they read *Julius Caesar*. He would have them learn punctuation as an extension of speech by asking them to transcribe dictation and write dialogue. For senior high and college students there is a spectrum of narrative types which wonderfully heightens awareness of informational and communicative processes in both real life and literature. As far as possible in all their work Mr. Moffett would have the students provide one another with feedback rather than receive it only from the teacher.

In this book the emphasis is on the frame of reference of a naturalistic language curriculum rather than upon detailed assignments (for the latter see Mr. Moffett's *A Student-Centered Language Arts Curriculum*). The author is agreeably diffident about his theories and wisely flexible in the advice he gives. His experience in teaching language is evident. He has a rare ability to see relations among language study, the curriculum as a whole and some of the general problems of our society. His goal is an exalted one: to enable the student "to play freely the whole symbolic scale."

ROGER BROWN

Harvard University

FOREWORD

THIS BOOK is addressed to teachers, other educators, and researchers in the many disciplines related to language learning. It comprises essays written while I was preparing *A Student-Centered Language Arts Curriculum, Grades K–13: A Handbook for Teachers,* to which it is meant to be a companion volume. Whereas the handbook proposes in some detail an experimental curriculum made up of particular practices and assignments for different ages, the present book sketches a pedagogical theory of discourse that may provide both a fuller rationale for the curriculum, if the reader is familiar with it, and, quite independently, a set of ideas to help advance the current task of reconceiving education in the native language. These essays represent one teacher's efforts to theorize about discourse expressly for teaching purposes. Whereas much that is of value has been said about the subject recently and in the past, very little theory has originated in a concern for how one *learns* to discourse. What follows in these pages must, as an individual endeavor, be very imperfect; the ideas await correction and completion by other minds.

Other minds, in fact, have already contributed considerably to these ideas. In the earlier stages of thought, William Schwarz, George Bennett, and Kenneth McElheny, former colleagues at Phillips Exeter Academy, helped me considerably to understand what I was trying to say. Associations with both the Society for General Semantics and the Institute of General Semantics provided very powerful stimulation for which I am much indebted. Fellow members of the School Language Group and other colleagues of the Harvard Graduate School of Education have filled in my knowledge and adjusted my thoughts in sorely needed ways.

Since all of this book but Chapters Five and Seven has been separately published, I am grateful to the following organizations for permission to reprint: The National Council of Teachers of English, The President and Fellows of Harvard University, The Society for General Semantics, The Yale Conference on English, and the New American Library. Individual acknowledgments and citations appear on appropriate pages of the text.

J.M.

CONTENTS

CHAPTER THREE

Drama: What Is Happening   60

CHAPTER FOUR

Narrative: What Happened   120

ture we reify it into substance. The form of one man's short story is the content of another man's critical essay. We begin by envisioning lines of force that magnetize a whole field and point the pedagogical way; then the first thing we know, we are beholding a mere "main idea" or "principle," which, even if it is new, is still a something like any other old piece of content and thus risks being treated the same old way. Any English teacher could drum up a grandiose thesis (such as, "Great literature reflects man's tragic conflict with himself"), illustrate it with selections from literature, and say that he had created a structural curriculum. I have four objections to this: it is old hat; it encourages a pre-digested, moralizing approach; it reveals more the structure of psychology and sociology than of literature; and even the structure of literature is not the structure of English. How, then, *do* we arrest the subtle transformation of structure into substance?

Anything is a structure. If we presuppose that some things are structures and other things are substantive elements which go into structures, we have trapped ourselves at the outset. Everything is both, which is to say that things and relations are matters of conceptual option. To understand the option one is playing one must be aware of where one has mentally placed himself. A tree is an element of a landscape, a thing, until we choose to isolate the tree, at which time it becomes a structure (if we talk about it at all) or set of relations among trunk, limbs, and branches. By calling something a structure, we mean that we are preferring to strip it of context, in fact to make it itself the context for some smaller structures. A molecule is a structure of atoms, which are structures of smaller "things," etc. A word is an element in a sentence, which is an element in a paragraph, which is an element in a composition. The physicist must consider his atom, the grammarian his sentence, as a structure, even though he knows perfectly well that in the next biggest context it is only a particle. In this "infinite regress of contexts," as Gregory Bateson has called it, elements stake out the field of vision, and relations among the elements rope it off; one does not see beyond, because "beyond" is where one is looking from.

Now, it is not hard to find *a* structure in English. All the particles — word, sentence, paragraph, compositional whole, literary "form" — offer us structures, a regress of increasingly larger contexts. But what are they *sub*-structures of? For the regress is only theoretically infinite; our conception is always finite. Some ultimate context or super-structure is exactly what English as a school subject has always lacked.

"English"

Untidy and amorphous as it is, "English" seems like a very unattractive candidate for a structural curriculum, which undoubtedly is a main reason for its being the caboose on the train of educational renovation. Sometimes it is defined as contents — literature, language, and composition (a non-parallel series if I ever saw one, since composition *ought* to be an activity). At other times it is defined as "arts" or skills — reading, writing, listening, speaking. (I think we should add thinking to this list.) Right away we confront the main dilemma, parallel to the dichotomy of substance and structure. How much is teaching English a matter of covering content, and how much a matter of developing skills, which are independent of any particular matter? Frequently the dilemma has been resolved by claiming that certain contents are essential to learning the skills. That is — to write one must know, as information, certain linguistic codifications and facts of composition; to read literature, one must be told about prosody and "form." But learning "form" this way is really learning content, and the result is quite different than if the student *practices* form or feels it invisibly magnetize the whole curriculum. *Learning* and *learning how to* result in very different kinds of knowledge. (Compare the psychiatrist's telling the patient, "You have an Oedipus complex," with the deep liberating reorganization that takes place gradually through the transference process.)

But, partly because it is easier to tell somebody than it is truly to lead him, partly because we assimilate English, by false analogy, to such subjects as history and science, we have misconstrued it and mistaught it. Although it is certainly the business of the English teacher to know as information the history and science of language and literature, it does not follow at all that he should teach these as contents to his elementary and secondary students. If he does teach, say, the history of literature or the science of language, organized as a corpus, he must justify doing so either on grounds that they improve certain skills or that they have value in their own right. Although some filling-in of historical context may be a reasonable adjunct to the reading of some works of literature, that is very different from organizing the whole literature course in historical-survey fashion or from assigning books of literary history. As for the science of language, the evidence from research indicates that teaching grammar, old-fashioned or new-fangled, has no effect on the skills. When I taught French I found that students did fine with *qui* and *que* until we got to the chapter that explained the difference, after which they constantly confused them. Certainly, on the other hand, we wouldn't deny that literary history and linguistics have value in themselves. But in this case a critical problem of priority arises. Why should physics be an elective and literary history required? Why offer linguistics in high school rather than psychology or anthropology, which might be deemed equally "basic"? The same problem exists for the science of literature and the history of language. I don't see how we can justify giving priority to the content specialties of English over those of other subjects, or teaching these specialties before students have thoroughly mastered the large English skills (there is a discouraging amount of evidence that this often doesn't occur even by the time of college). If one does believe that skills pre-empt contents in English, then a structural curriculum is already in sight, for teaching functionally, teaching *how to,* keeps the operating relations of the field from becoming things.

Today the approach is far too substantive. Take up practically any textbook on language or composition and you will find it organized in this way: categories, and therefore units of study, are derived by analytically decomposing language into the "elements." This is what I call the particle approach — sound, perhaps, for research, but not for teaching. Although this approach pays lip service to the interrelations of elements, it cannot escape its own format. To cash in on current slogans like "sequential development," publishers often arrange these particles in an order of smaller to larger — from the word to the sentence to the paragraph to the whole composition. I do not know what development this corresponds to — certainly not to the functioning of either the language or the student. For one thing, only in the largest context — the whole composition — can meaning, style, logic, or rhetoric be usefully contemplated. Secondly, little particle to big particle is not even an order of simple to complex, since each sub-structure is as complex as the next largest. What *does* count is that, as context for the next smallest, each of these structures governs everything of significance in the one below. For the same reasons, units on style, logic, and rhetoric can teach little more than abstract information if these things are not kept as functions of each other, and they can be kept so only in the ultimate context of somebody-talking-to-somebody-else-about-something.

To the extent the English teacher has an obligation to familiarize the student with what has been written in the past, he rightly has a problem of content-coverage. But any approach that entailed plenty of reading could accomplish this. We no longer agree very much on what every gentleman ought to have read, and the survey of literature seems to have placed us more in the role of historian than we thought appropriate. Virtually any curriculum could sample the range of literature. Genre divisions satisfy a passion for taxonomy. Though perhaps the best classification of literature so far, genres are too cavalierly equated with form and structure. Actually, the structure of a novel or play is at least as much unique to itself as it is shared by other novels and plays. And some stories are poems, some poems stories, some plays essays, and some essays are stories or poems. Perhaps more than anything else, genres are marketing directives. As such, they provide convenient rhetorical bins. Pedagogically, they constitute a hazard by making both teachers and students feel that they have to "define" what a short story or a poem is, i.e., find something similar in all the examples. Even if this were not futile, one would be left with only a definition, another substantive reduction that does not help one to read or write, or even appreciate. Since a definition would have to be of the form, not content, the very difficulty of definition suggests that we exaggerate greatly the formal similarities among members of the same genre.

At the risk of disparaging what a lot of English teachers, including myself, have relied on as curriculum guides, I have emphasized the ways we have unnecessarily deformed our subject to make it into a content like other subjects. But English, mathematics, and foreign languages are not *about* anything in the same sense that history, biology, physics, and other primarily empirical subjects are about something. English, French, and mathematics are *symbol systems,* into which the phenomenal data of empirical subjects are cast and by means of which we think about them. Symbol systems are not primarily about themselves; they are about other subjects. When a student "learns" one of these systems, he *learns how to* operate it. The main point is to think and talk about other things by means of this system.

In insisting on a major division between symbol systems and what is symbolized in the systems, I am attempting to break up the bland surface of our traditional curriculum, whereby the Carthaginian Wars, the theorems of Euclid, irregular German verbs, the behavior of amoebas, and the subordination of clauses all come dead-level across the board if they were the same kind of knowledge. The failure to distinguish *kinds* and *orders* of knowledge amounts to a crippling epistemological error built into the very heart of the overall curriculum. The classification by "subject matters" into English, history, math, science, French, etc., implies that they are all merely contents that differ only in what they are about. The hidden assumptions of this classification have taught students to be naïve about both symbols and the nature of information; even very bright students are apt to leave high school not understanding the difference between empirical truth and logical validity. Furthermore, we have fooled ourselves.

Fortunately, the curriculum builders of mathematics and foreign languages have made some progress in overcoming this confusion. They have done so by reconceiving their subjects in terms of relations and skills. The most natural assumption about teaching any symbol system should be that the student employ his time using that system in every realistic way that it can be used, not that he analyze it or study it as an object. (In this respect an English curriculum would not differ basically from any other first-language curriculum; what I have to say in this essay applies as well to French for the French or Russian for the Russians.) If such an approach seems to slight literature and language, I can only say that this is a mistake of the substantive view. A student writing in all the same forms as the authors he reads can know literature from the inside in a way that few students ever do today. If the student has to work with language constantly in the functional way the professional does, he will come to know it in the professional's intimate way. Through reading, writing, and discussing whole, authentic discourses — and using no textbooks — students can learn better everything that we consider of value in language and literature than they can by the current substantive and particle approach.

As it is now, I see us turning out glib Advanced Placement students who know all the critical jargon and can talk about writing endlessly, but who do not write well and are not truly sensitive to style, rhetoric, and logic. In many of our writing assignments, I see us feverishly searching for subjects for students to write about that are *appropriate for English;* so we send them to the libraries to paraphrase encyclopedias, or they re-tell the plots of books, or they write canned themes on moral or literary topics for which no honest student has any motivation. Although asking students to write about real life as they know it is gaining ground, still many teachers feel such assignments are vaguely "permissive" and not as relevant as they ought to be. Once we acknowledge that "English" is not properly about itself, then a lot of phoney assignments and much of the teacher's confusion can go out the window. Speaking as one of many university professors who have to stop and teach their graduate students to write, Wendell Johnson has relieved his exasperation in this way:

> The second, and more grave, reason for their [English teachers'] failure is that they appear to place the emphasis on "writing," rather than on writing-about-something-for-someone. You cannot write writing.[1]

Johnson catches here just my point about teachers feeling that they have to do "English" about English. Clearly distinguishing symbolizing subjects from symbolized subjects would eliminate such nonsense.

Having said this, however, I must now enter a great paradox: in trying to separate symbol from symbolized, one discovers their inseparability. Ultimately, we cannot free data from the symbols into which they have been abstracted, the message from the code. All knowledge is some codification by man of his phenomenal world. This is precisely what many incoming college freshmen and even graduate students have never learned. The fact is that languages *are* about themselves, in a greater measure than we usually suspect; but this is a wholly different matter from the English teacher's fear that if he does not keep English self-contained it will slip through his fingers and become as big as all outdoors. The ambiguity I am after is that while we speak in English about non-English things, we are using invisible syntactic relations as well as words like "although" and "because" that are not about the phenomenal world — at least not the external one. Every code or language says something about itself while delivering its message. According to communications engineers, codification is the substitution of one set of events for another. The set of events which we substitute for outer phenomena when we talk about them is an inner set of neural events — activities we learn when we learn

[1] "You Can't Write Writing," S. I. Hayakawa, ed., *The Use and Misuse of Language* (New York: Fawcett Publications, Inc., 1962), p. 109.

the language and about which we are normally unaware. The purpose, I take it, of teaching linguistics and semantics is to make the student aware of how much people's words are about people and words and how much they truly recapitulate outer phenomena. But this is best done by letting students *try* to symbolize raw phenomena of all kinds at all levels of abstraction, and then by discussing these efforts under the guidance of a teacher who is linguistically and semantically sophisticated. I think it will be found that what we might tell the student or have him read about concerning the reflexiveness of language will be much better learned through his own writing and discussion. By this method, teachers may more readily learn what kind of understanding of language the student can take at different ages and in what form they can take it.

Yes, language is about itself, but, in accordance with something like Russell's theory of types, higher abstractions are about lower abstractions, never about themselves. That is, some English words refer to the outer world, other words (like relative pronouns) refer to these first words, and all syntax is about tacit rules for putting together the concrete words. Some notion of a hierarchy of abstraction, defined as greater and greater processing of phenomena by the human mind, is indispensable. Thus, the more abstract language is, the more it is meta-language, culminating in mathematics as the ultimate language about language. So we imagine a symbolic hierarchy going from the codification of our world that most nearly reflects the structure of that world to codification that more and more resembles the structure of the mind. Basically this is what abstraction is all about. To enable the student to learn about this process, we must first separate in the curriculum, and hence in the student's mind, symbolic systems from empirical subjects, and then help him discover both the dependence and independence of one and the other.

I hope it is clear at this point that I am construing English as all discourse in our native language — any verbalizing of any phenomena, whether thought, spoken, or written; whether literary or non-literary. Seen as packets of heterogeneous content, on the one hand, and as skills on the other, English does indeed seem unwieldy and resistant to structure. But if we smelt back down to the simplest relations of discourse all substantive categories, we may be able to re-cast the curriculum so as to accommodate all that we agree is important.

The Structure of Discourse

The elements of discourse are a first person, a second person, and a third person; a speaker, listener, and subject; informer, informed, and information; narrator, auditor, and story; transmitter, receiver, and message. The structure of discourse, and therefore the super-structure of English, is this set of relations among the three persons. But in order to exploit this venerable trinity, we must get beyond its innocent look.

Within the relation of the speaker to his listener lie all the issues by which we have recently enlarged the meaning of "rhetoric" — what A wishes to do by speaking of such and such a subject to B. Within the relation of the speaker to his subject lie all the issues of the abstractive process — how the speaker has symbolically processed certain raw phenomena. But of course these two relations are in turn related: *what* and *what for* are factors of each other. As with all trinities, the relations of persons is a unity — somebody-talking-to-somebody-about something. And, lastly, within the relation of the listener to the subject lie all the issues which we call comprehension and interpretation.

In proposing this structure, I am thinking that the student would learn the skills of operating our symbol system by role-playing first and second persons in all the possible relations that might exist between the student and a subject, and between him and a speaker or listener. For the set of relations is of course not static, and, as the ultimate context, this structure governs the variations in style, logic, and rhetoric of all the sub-structures beneath it — the word, the sentence, the paragraph, and the compositional or literary "form." This amounts to proposing that curriculum units and sequence be founded on different kinds of discourse, a "discourse" being defined as any piece of verbalization complete for its original purpose. What creates different kinds of discourse are shifts in the relations among persons — increasing rhetorical distance between speaker and listener, and increasing abstractive altitude between the raw matter of some subject and the speaker's symbolization of it.

There is one thing that no grammar book will ever tell us about the trinity of discourse: first and second persons are of a different order of reality than third person. Whereas *I* and *you* are existential, unabstracted persons, *he* or *it* has merely referential or symbolic reality. That is, *I* and *you* inhabit some space-time, but, in a given communication situation, *he* or *it* inhabits only the timeless realm of abstraction. Thus if Tom and Dick want to exclude Harry, even if he is standing right before them, all they have to do is *refer to him.* This says clearly, "You do not exist in the same way we do." When the servant addresses His Highness, he uses the third person to deny the actual *I-you* relation and thereby maintain the discontinuity of their realities. Perhaps — in a somewhat simplified sense — Martin Buber's distinction between an *I-it* relation and an *I-thou* relation best expresses the two different orders of reality. That is, when something or somebody is an *it* for me, I am manipulating the idea of them I have in my head, which is to say that I am relating only to myself; whereas when something or somebody is a *thou* for me, I am meeting directly their unabstracted, existential reality, which is independent of me and equal to me. Buber rightly associates the *I-it* relation with verbal, discursive, scientific knowing, and the *I-thou* relation with non-symbolic meeting or action. This corresponds in the structure of discourse to the abstractive relation between first and third persons and the rhetorical relation between first and second persons.

My reason for establishing this difference in kind of reality is that it helps us clarify the innocent opaqueness of the conceptual scheme of "persons" so that we can better discriminate between the action relation of human-to-human and the symbolic relation of human-to-referent. *I* and *you* pre-empt the communication process, just as transmitter and receiver exist before message, although they are defined as such only by virtue of sending and receiving messages. The starting point, then, of teaching discourse is "drama": interaction between the communicants, who are equal and whose relation is reversible. (Within a given communication situation, *I* and *it* cannot reverse roles.) One failure of English teaching has been to consider only messages, or consider them before or without placing them in the whole context of the communication frame wherein the student can see the operation of all relations.

Viewing the student for a moment as an *I* asked to write something, let's think about *what* and *what for*. His *what* does not usually entail his abstracting raw phenomena from the ground up, and as for his *what for* — his motivation for writing the theme, his audience, and how he wishes to act on that audience — we find slim pickings indeed. He is writing always to the same old person, the English teacher, to whom he has nothing to say but who has given him a *what for* by demanding the assignment and by holding the power of grades and disciplinary authority over him. No wonder that what he learns most is to dope out the idiosyncracies of the teacher and give him what he wants — a fine lesson in rhetoric which Harold Martin once called somewhere the "nice-Nelly" school of writing. While acknowledging that artificiality cannot be eliminated completely from the classroom situation, somehow we must create more realistic communication "dramas" in which the student can practice being a first and second person with better motivation and in a way more resembling how he will have to read, write, speak, and listen in the "afterlife." I recommend training the student to write for the class group, which is the nearest thing to a contemporary world-at-large; accustoming him to having his themes read and discussed workshop fashion; and asking him to write about raw material from his own experience which he is motivated to write about and to invent an appropriate rhetoric for. It is amazing how much so-called writing problems clear up when the student really cares, when he is realistically put into the drama of somebody with something to say to somebody else.

I have suggested structuring English curriculum according to the relations of speaker-listener-subject as the ultimate context within which all our other concerns may be handled functionally and holistically, moving the student in his writing and reading from one kind of actual discourse to the next in a sequence which permits him to learn style, logic, semantics, rhetoric, and literary form continuously through practice as first or second person. Ideally this sequence would correspond both to his own intellectual and emotional growth and to some significant progression in "symbolic transformation," as Suzanne Langer has called the human processing of the world. The structure of the subject must be meshed with the structure of the student. A major failure of education has been to consider the logic of the one almost to the exclusion of the psychologic of the other. To paraphrase Earl Kelley, we build the right facilities, organize the best course of study, work out the finest methods, create the appropriate materials, and then, come September, the wrong students walk through the door. Atomizing a subject into analytical categories, inherent only in the subject, necessarily slights the internal processes of the student or language-user, who in any given instance of an authentic discourse is employing all the sub-structures, working in all the categories, at once. We must re-conceive the subject in such a way that we can talk simultaneously about both the operations of the field and the operations of the learner. The title of a paper by Warren McCulloch expresses splendidly this transactional approach: "What Is A Number, That A Man May Know It, and A Man, That He May Know A Number?" We should ask the same question regarding our native language. What assures me that a correspondence is possible between phases of discourse and stages of growth is that all man's artifacts reflect him, and discourse is man-made. I think that in exploring all the shifts that can occur in the rhetorical relation of *I-you* and the abstractive relation of *I-it*, we will find sequences of activities that can be embodied in a curriculum doing justice to both learned and learner. But it is only in the largest context — any instance of a whole, authentic discourse — that the nature of the two can meet. The concept that seems most likely to enable us to think simultaneously about discourse and the learning of discourse is that of abstraction, redefined so as to apply to whole discourses and the rhetorical process behind them.

language, is a matter of translating inner reality into the public terms of the subject.

The chief difficulty with this strategy is the lack of information about how the thought and speech of children do in fact grow. Whereas theories of grammar, rhetoric, and literature can flourish in relative independence of psychological information, theories of child development depend largely on empirical research. Most of what we know today about this development is vague, controversial, and hard to translate into a curriculum. What I would like to do here is piece together a theory of verbal and cognitive growth in terms of the school subject, basing it partly on present knowledge but definitely going beyond what can be proven. A comprehensive rationale for a learning sequence in language may never be provable, but the practices suggested by the rationale can certainly be tested in schools for their efficacy, and some hypothesis is necessary even to acquire more knowledge. In our ignorance we still have to make assumptions for further research and for an interim curriculum sequence. The theory of discourse that makes up most of this chapter is meant to be utilized, not believed. I am after a strategic gain in concept.

Language and Cognition

At the outset let me try to remove a possible source of confusion and at the same time explain why I believe language learning is ultimately a cognitive matter. Both reading and writing are at once shallow mechanical activities and deep operations of mind and spirit. There is no necessary connection between reading and the comprehension of words, or between writing and composition. Comprehending and composing are independent of written symbols. The basic problems of understanding what someone else says to us, or of putting thoughts into words, can and should be separated from mere decoding of letters and mere transcribing of speech, which involve only perceptual and motor skills, not thought and emotion. One could learn to read aloud and take dictation, as did Milton's daughters, without knowing what the words meant. We acknowledge the independence of composition from print when we speak of oral composition and oral literature. And problems of reading comprehension are simply problems of comprehension; if a text were heard instead of read, the ideas would be no easier to understand, given that the reader knew how to recapitulate voice from a page. And *that* is the chief learning issue at the mechanical level — tying letters to vocal sounds and punctuation to intonation.

The distinction between literal and conceptual levels is obvious, but equally obvious is that we often forget it. For example, a common curriculum assumption is that spelling and punctuation should continue to be taught beyond primary school, whereas this mere transcriptive skill is not developmental beyond the age of around nine. I can't imagine what further maturation taking place beyond then would enable a student to learn more about the relations between print and speech if he had not already learned them. No new powers of conception have to be waited upon. Expansion of vocabulary will not introduce new sound-letter relationships. Further conversational and reading experience may introduce more complex sentence structures but no new principle for punctuating them. Why, then, do we still have to teach spelling, punctuation, and elemental reading to children beyond the age of nine or ten? There may be several reasons, but none concerns normal maturation. Except for some new words that cannot be spelled from phonics understanding alone, all teaching of decoding and transcribing skills beyond this age must be considered remedial. In other words, we continue to teach these things only because we did not succeed in teaching them before, not because students were not developed enough to learn them. If, at the outset, punctuation were taught by speech intonation, and if the sound-letter relationships were taught thoroughly through writing as well as reading, we might well find that teachers beyond the middle years of elementary school would be free to concentrate on the truly developmental issues of mental and emotional growth. In contrast to decoding and transcribing, comprehending and composing do indeed evolve as children mature.

Look at it this way. We have meanings, vocal sounds symbolizing those meanings, and written marks symbolizing the vocal sounds. Rendering vocalization and intonation into graphic signs, and vice versa, is merely matching an auditory symbol system with a visual symbol system. This means, as Vygotsky for one pointed out, that reading and writing are a second-degree abstraction — symbols for symbols — but by school age or before, children seem ready for this second layer of symbols, and learning the regular relations between them is a mechanical matter of pairing associations. It is the matching of symbols to referents that is truly difficult and developmental. Meanings cannot be merely paired off with words by rules of regularity. But most of all, referents are concepts of things, and both our concepts and our ways of interrelating them change as we grow. In recent experiments,[1] Piaget has found that children recalling a design shown to them once could more accurately represent it six months later, in pictures or in words, than they could only a week later, when their memory should have been fresher. He attributes this to the interim development of their ability to cognize and symbolize, since obviously they perceived the design just as accurately at the time of its presentation but could not then show that they did. Moreover, the work of one of his colleagues, Hermina Sinclair-de Zwart, seems to indicate that teaching of language forms cannot hasten this ability to represent reality more accurately.[2] These experiments point up, I

[1] See *On the Development of Memory and Identity* (Barre, Mass.: Barre Publishers, 1967), two Heinz Werner memorial lectures delivered by Piaget at Clark University.

[2] In *Langage et Opérations — Sous-système linguistique et opérations concrètes* (Paris: Dunod, 1967) Hermina Sinclair-de Zwart reports several experiments in which children's language performance was matched against their performance on certain conservation and seriation tasks involving physical operations. She found that the possession of linguistic terms and structures was neither necessary nor sufficient for performing these cognitive tasks, and that teaching the children the relevant verbal formulations influenced little their performance on the conservation tasks. She concludes that some general laws of psychological development govern the parallel growth of language and operations, so that even if language acquisition seems to run somewhat ahead, as it did sometimes in these experiments, it cannot really outstrip or hasten cognitive growth. Although the imitation of verbal models plays

believe, the fact that development of symbolic expression depends on nothing less than general mental growth.

Abstraction

The concept that I believe will most likely permit us to think at once about both mental development and the structure of discourse is the concept of abstraction, which can apply equally well to thought and to language. My effort here will be to make a very qualified equation between levels of abstraction and stages of growth.

I have said that the superstructure of discourse is the set of relations among speaker, listener, and subject — first, second, and third persons. The *I–it* relation concerns information — how someone abstracts *from raw phenomena*. The *I–you* relation concerns communication — how someone abstracts *for an audience*. The first is the referential relation; the second is the rhetorical relation. Although the informative and communicative aspects of discourse cannot in reality be separated, for conceptual purposes they may. I would like to take first the *I–it* relationship, abstracting *from*. It will involve us in information-processing, the transforming of matter into mind, cognizing. Of course "transforming" is only a metaphor. Raw phenomena remain forever themselves, unspeakable, regardless of how much we abstract them. Not all abstraction, furthermore, is verbal. But if we keep these restrictions in mind, we may proceed safely.

In common and technical parlance, the words "abstraction" and "to abstract" seem to refer to both the abstracting and the abstracted and, as the following sentences illustrate, to apply in what appear to be very different domains. "The individual *abstracts* objects from his environment" (perception). "This student has chosen to write on a more *abstract* subject than that student ("size" of referent). "The concept of bartering is easier than the concept of international trade because the latter is

an undeniably large role in language learning, she says, the functional use the child makes of language as an instrument of thought depends on his operational needs.

more *abstract*" (concept formation). "Proposition two about proposition one is of a higher order of *abstraction* than proposition one" (logic). This diversity of usage might indicate that abstraction is an overly loose and unworkable concept, but I prefer to believe that it indicates a similarity of process underlying all stages of information-processing, from sensori-motor and perceptual to affective and intellectual. At each stage, abstraction means something a little different but it still retains stable meaning through all stages — which is an excellent reason for our using "abstraction" to cover so many different phenomena.

One element of abstraction is the ranging of the mind's materials in *hierarchies* of classes and sub-classes, superordinates and subordinates. The class concept "international trade" is more abstract than its subordinate class concept "bartering." Similarly "mammals" includes "dogs." But what about "international trade" and "dog," which do not belong to the same hierarchy? If these were the respective subjects of two student themes, we would probably consider the first to be a more abstract topic than the second. How so? I think the answer is that we form a rough notion of equivalent altitude between concepts in different hierarchies. We speak of levels of abstraction and assign "international trade" to a higher level and "dog" to a lower one, even though the two concepts are of different classification systems. If asked to rank "international trade" and "parabolic trajectory" we would probably be hard put to assign one a level higher than another. (I would be pleased if the reader were to dispute this.)

What intuition underlies this rough assigning of levels when one class cannot logically include another as a sub-class? It seems to me we use as a yardstick the extension in time and space of the referent. For example, one could observe an instance of "bartering" or of "dog" by standing at one point in space-time, but one could not so observe an instance of "international trade," which is itself a complex of actions occurring at different times and places. "Concreteness," the traditional antonym for "abstractness," is a matter of just this extension of the referent in time and space. So to the notion of class inclusion we can add this definition of concreteness. "Pop fly" is both more concrete than "parabolic trajectory" and is a sub-class of it. In fact, "parabolic trajectory" is superordinate *because* it has as referent something more removed from the particular circumstance of ball, bat, and baseball field. Its instances are its sub-classes, that is, intangible or mental entities whose instances are in turn things observable at a certain time and place.

A second element in abstraction is selection — constructing in one's mind an object out of the indivisible phenomenal world by singling out some environmental features and ignoring others. As Alfred Korzybski never tired of pointing out, we can never abstract *all* the features of our surroundings. First of all, our attention itself is selective; we notice what we need and want to notice and what we have learned to notice. Secondly, even of those things our attention settles on we can only register a few features, for two reasons: our receptors are limited, and our prior gestalts dictate what is significant and what is not. To approach perceptual selectivity — low-level abstraction — I resort again to the communication engineers' definition of coding — the substitution of one set of events for another. When something is coded from one medium to another, the coding must partake of the qualities of the second medium, which can never reproduce all the qualities of the first. All our sensory receptors can do is *simulate,* electrochemically, the external phenomena they are registering. To see a leaf is not to incorporate it, nor literally to transform it (the leaf remains the same), but rather to create in our body a representation of it that is structurally similar to it. A television image is a lineal coding into successive emissions which are later recoded into a two-dimensional arrangement of electrons. Conversely, our vision of the leaf is spatially represented in our retinal structure, then recoded into a succession of neural impulses to the brain. Our perception, moreover, is hardly pure; although not limited like the frog to seeing only a few genetically determined silhouettes, we do impose our gestalts at the very moment of perceiving. Looking is rare. We look at and look for. In short, in substituting inner events for outer events we automatically edit reality. Information is lost, and it is hard to know what features we are missing. Think, for one example, of the frequencies of sound and light radiation that our receptors are simply not built to pick up. And three-dimensionality is something only a combination of several receptors and our body movements can make apparent to us.

Memory, or recalled perception, selects features at a higher level. What is involved is not just fading of detail; many affective and cognitive factors determine what "left an impression" and what "stands out." From a later point of view, one categorizes and interprets events, partly in the light of new information received in the interim. But most of all, the details of a particular scene "stick" because they become assimilated to similar details from other scenes remote in time from that one. The linking of perceptions of different times and places may be affective or logical. Whether the link is a fear feeling or the gestalt of rectangularity or the notion of fair play, something we can call a category has been formed, and the detail in question is recallable because it is associated with analogous memories, all serving as instances of the category.

Memory operates by and leads to classes and class concepts. The problem with these terms is that they suggest rational, public, conscious categorizations of experience, whereas it is clear from mental illness, intuitive creativity, and interpersonal disagreement that many of our "classes" and "concepts" are irrational, private, and unconscious. The point, in any case, is that whether the generalization is about "what I can and cannot do" or about the similarities among "pop fly," "path of artillery shell," and "course of thrown rock," a great reductive summary has taken place of prior perceptions and memories. Selecting and ignoring are at the heart of such summary. "Parabolic trajectory" ignores bat, cannon, and rock and fastens only on the kind of course produced by any projectile under any circumstance as it overcomes and then submits to gravity. In this case the category is publicly recognized and named, and the verbal learning of this category undoubtedly facilitates the linking and lumping together of perceptions. In the case of a person whose self-concept prescribes and proscribes certain behavior, the category may well be unconscious and private. He has nonetheless generalized "what I can do" and "what I can't do" by seeing in a number of separate events evidence of the same fact. To do this he ignores other features of the events. By thus summarizing his experience he can, or feels he can, better guide his future actions.

Selection is very subtle. Although it often seems like simple elimination, it means something somewhat different at different levels of the nervous system. Even in perception it does not happen by removing some features and leaving the others unchanged, as if one were to remove several items from a store window display and leave the other items just as they were. What happens — in different ways with perception, memory and ratiocination — is that the features are not only selected but *reorganized,* and, increasingly as we go up the scale of the nervous system, *integrated with previously abstracted information.* Thus selection occurs as part of a larger process of digestion and assimilation. Whereas in perception, it is sensory data that are being selected and rearranged in relation to each other, in memory and generalization, it is the lower-order abstractions themselves that are selected. That is, the "matter" being reduced is increasingly the inner codings and not the external stimuli. Abstraction is "higher" as it is more reflexive — one neural operation integrating prior neural operations. More and more, the "subject" is internal and farther removed from outside phenomena; the referents are other abstractions.

What then of "propositions one and two"? In what sense is a statement about a statement more abstract? The referent of P_2 is an item like P_2 itself, another proposition — not a class of things and not material things themselves. This represents the extreme degree of symbolic reflexiveness, of metalinguistic involution. But P_2 is "higher" than P_1 because it *refers to* P_1. A symbol is always more abstract than its referent, i.e. represents yet another step of mentation. P_2 is a further thought about P_1.

A definition of abstraction, in sum, must center on a notion of selection; but this selection, as it operates through perception, memory, and generalization, implies some reorganization of features according to the nature of the apparatus doing the selecting and according to previous knowledge systems that have grown in the organism. A definition must also include the notion of hierarchy and hierarchical integration — of orders of symbolization and stages of internal processing. The combining of propositions cannot take place until classes exist, and classes depend on the categorizing of experience, which presupposes memories of perceptions. Abstraction, by selecting and ranking the elements of experience, reduces reality to manageable summaries. To abstract is to trade a loss of reality for a gain in control.

Abstraction and Curriculum

Whenever I ask people to define abstraction for me, they resort finally to talking about how people, especially, children, learn. It is hard to avoid an analogy between stages of information processing that go on in all of us all the time, and developmental stages of growth. A curriculum sequence based on such an analogy, however, needs to be carefully qualified. Although developmental research often suggests that cognitive growth moves in the direction of higher abstracting, such as logical operations, a lot of evidence implies that even very small children make rather high-level inferences, although it is doubtful that they "think out" such inferences as adults might. The linguists, for example, are very impressed — properly, I think — by the generalization entailed in the child's competence in creating structurally well-formed sentences that he has never heard before. From the data provided by other people's sentences he infers some working model of syntax before he enters school. But let's take another sort of example. At a parents' meeting of a nursery school my daughter was attending, a father told about his five-year-old son's refusal to eat, which was becoming a serious problem until one night, in an unguarded moment at the supper table, as if speaking to himself, the child said, "If you eat, you grow up to be big and strong — and die." With rare explicitness he had verbalized the perfectly logical but usually unconscious kind of thinking that underlies a lot of children's behavior. The boy had combined two generalizations — premise one, that eating makes you grow up, and premise two, that growing older means approaching death — and concluded, with splendid syllogistic sense, that to eat is to die. Because he revealed his logic, the boy's parents could point out that if you don't eat, you die even sooner. But how much of children's inexplicable behavior is based on similar buried abstracting? The fact that the cognitive distortions known as mental illness originate so often in childhood suggests that a lot of abstracting goes on at that age, however unconscious and sub-verbal it may be. There is every reason to believe that a child puts his perceptions and memories together so as to form categories of experience, and that on the basis of these categories he makes some generalizations and syllogisms about the world and himself.

A child is not an empty vessel when he enters school; he comes replete with a set of abstractions about the world and himself, some of which he may have acquired ready-made from others but some of which he generated himself from his own experience. It is these latter that are troublesome to others, obscure to himself, and not very amenable to influence and possible correction. They are unconscious, private, and essentially non-verbal (they sound verbal only because we have to denote them with language). Yet they determine a lot of his behavior. And control of behavior becomes possible only as awareness of these abstractions arises. In short, increased *consciousness* of abstracting has as much to do with developmental growth as has progression up the abstraction ladder. I believe that growth along one dimension fosters growth along the other. This would square with Piaget's insistence on decreasing egocentrism as a dimension of growth. That is, certain cognitive processes which we associate with higher abstraction may become possible only as the child becomes aware that he is abstracting. Because higher abstracting is so much about lower abstractions, it may be impossible to make inferences of a certain generality and complexity without becoming aware of prior stages. Or the effort to make such inferences may of itself induce this awareness. Also, words seem necessary to higher abstraction and this necessitates greater consciousness.

With this qualification in mind, that the consciousness of abstracting may relate reciprocally to the growth of abstracting, it seems reasonable to propose a curriculum based on the hierarchy of abstraction. And my idea would be to have such a curriculum recapitulate, in successive assignments, the abstractive stages across which all of us all the time symbolize raw phenomena and manipulate these symbolizations. Not only do we grow slowly through the whole abstractive range during our period of maturation, but at any time of life we are constantly processing new experience up through the cycle of sensations, memories, generalizations, and theories.

The essential purpose of such a curriculum would be to have the student abstract at all ranges of the symbolic spectrum and progressively to integrate his abstractions into thought structures that assimilate both autistic and public modes of cognition. The hypothesis is that speaking, writing, and reading in forms of discourse that are successively more abstract makes it possible for the learner to understand better what is entailed at each stage of the hierarchy, to relate one stage to another, and thus to become aware of how he and others create information and ideas. The goal is not so much to attain the higher levels as it is to practice abstracting all along the way. No greater value is ascribed to one level than to another. Both concreteness and abstraction are dangerous and valuable. Increasingly, in the future, people will need to know, not how to store and retrieve information, which can be done by machines, but what the nature of information is and how it can be best abstracted. This is why, ultimately, substance is less important in English than structure. To be the master, and not the dupe, of symbols, the symbol-maker must understand the nature and value of his abstractions. This takes consciousness and an integrated view of the hierarchical, inner processing.

I am not talking here just about dry data and intellectual matters. I am trying to talk simultaneously about effective thought, emotional health, and active values. The relations among feeling, thought, and values are such that this course seems not only possible but in the end necessary. Psychological disorders are, as much as anything else, cognitive disorders. Autistic, syncretic, unconscious, primary-process symbolizing is just as much abstracting as the public, logical, and verbal symbolizing of secondary process. It is not that one is at the bottom of the hierarchy and the other at the top; both may operate within a large range of the abstraction spectrum. But the former is less open to inspection, less under control, less subject to alteration. And it exerts great influence on the cognition that *is* visible and controllable. For all its subjectivity, a category of "people who will hurt me" is just as much a class-concept, or abstraction of experience, as "international trade"; it too subsumes a number of particular happenings at different times and places (memories of perceptions). "Younger sisters get all the attention" is just as much a general proposition as "A common feature of family life is sibling rivalry." Too often we deem less abstract an idea that is merely less publicly valid. Also, autistic classes and propositions are apt not to be verbalized or consciously "thought" but rather to be expressed in systematic behavior. Such operating generalizations should really be deemed abstractions; otherwise we risk denying something we know, which is that not all cognition is conscious and verbal. Again, the awesome ability of small children to create novel sentences modelled on a paradigm they are unconscious of demonstrates a very powerful operating generalization which they have somehow "inferred" from instances of others' sentences and which they practice in their vocal behavior. Why would they not bring this faculty to bear on the other data of their experience?

The relation of abstraction to value is contained in the word "preference." To abstract is to select and ignore; to value is also to give priority to some things over others, to prefer. Among the claims various stimuli make upon us, we must choose. Among the alternatives for action that we associate with these stimuli, we must choose. Though our conditioning is so potent as to make "choice" a mere irony at first, I believe it is possible to open up for the young the repertory of options among what can be seen, what can be made of what is seen, and what, consequently, can be done. Our behavior is very dependent on our information, on what we think is so and what we think the meaning of something is. The more one becomes conscious of his own abstracting, the more he understands that his information is relative and can be enlarged and modified. By perceiving, inferring, and interpreting differently, he enlarges his behavioral repertory, sees new possible courses of action, and knows better why he is acting as he does. Choice becomes more real. The function of informing is essentially to guide action. Although we do at times, when free of decision-making, abstract in a spirit of play or of pure curiosity, what we shouldn't forget is that abstracting, like breathing, goes on all the time for the chief purpose of ensuring that we will survive and prevail. Notoriously, we see and interpret according to our needs and desires. Our values are the ways we believe we can fulfill these needs and desires. But a need to feel powerful, for example, can be fulfilled any number of ways; which ways we choose — the values we will live by, our preferences — will depend in large measure on what we "know" about what is relevant and possible. In both abstracting and valuing, the dark issue is what we did *not* select. Do we know there are other features, other inferences, other courses of action? Is a style or a value merely a conditioned reflex, or an election from a large array?

I am convinced that a very large measure of what educators mean by "teaching students to think" is in reality making them conscious of abstracting but is, unfortunately, seldom viewed this way. A salutary approach is to conceive the task as learning how to re-think or un-think. If a student becomes aware of his abstractive process by discoursing progressively up the hierarchy, and by examining his discourses in collaboration with peers and a guiding adult, he has an opportunity to correct and adjust his cognition. Josh Billings once said that people's problems come not so much from their ignorance as from knowing so many things that are not so. A student, even at age six, knows an enormous amount that isn't so, or that is at least severely limited. His intellectual growth will be more a liberation than an acquisition. An undeveloped nervous system, accidental association of events, the Freudian "family drama," the natural egocentrism of the inexperienced — all contribute to his abstracting ineffectual models of the world and himself. Most of his life will be spent in finding out the hard way that there are other ways of abstracting and that his is private and parochial. That is, most bright ideas he will have later will be an unthinking of what he long felt was a certainty. Most creative breakthroughs and dramatic scientific advances consist of just this kind of revision or rethinking. Copernicus and Galileo had to *remove* an idea; that was their new thought. Einstein had to crash through the culture's "current abstractions," to use Whitehead's phrase. In this sense, a new thought is a further thought about an old one. An abstraction does not get revised except by abstracting about it at a higher level, that is, at a stage of knowledge integration that has broader perspective than that from which the original abstraction was created.

Ideally, a student would spend his time in a language course of study abstracting a large amount of raw material into categories of experience and then into propositions which finally he would combine so as to arrive at new propositions not evident at any of the lower stages. By discussing his productions in a workshop class, he could profit from other points of view, discover what part of his abstracting is peculiar to him and what he shares with a public, and see how the worth of his higher abstractions is determined by the worth of his lower ones. Generally, a student should learn to play freely the whole symbolic scale, and to know where he is on it at a given moment. Most of our faulty thinking, and consequently a lot of our ineffective behavior, come from confusing abstraction levels and assigning to a high-order inference the same truth value we assign to a lower-order "factual" abstraction about which public agreement would be high. The key is the consciousness of abstracting — as general semanticists have insisted for years. This consciousness is worth more than all the courses in logic because it is something any logician, amateur or professional, stands no chance without. It grows slowly over the years, but different conditions can retard or advance it.

But how do we chart growth across the abstractive hierarchy? Does a child merely climb the ladder slowly over the years? No, for growth is more intricate than that. Embryology provides the best metaphor: a simple cell becomes a complex organism by differentiating itself into specialized parts at the same time that it maintains integrity by continually interrelating these parts. Mental growth, too, consists of two simultaneous progressions — toward differentiation and toward integration. We build our knowledge structures upward and downward at the same time. A child frequently over-abstracts as well as under-abstracts: he cuts his world into a few simple categories that cover too much and discriminate too little, and that display no subordinate or superordinate relations among themselves. Or he makes a generalization that is too broad for the meager experience it is based on. He fails to qualify and quantify his statements. Judging only by the surface generality of his words and sentences, one would conclude that he was thinking at a high level of abstraction. But he may be understanding "international trade" as "barter," not as the complex of activities adults understand by the word. That is, he may use early many concepts that only later will take on the meaning adults give to them. And his concepts are all ranged in his mind on the same plane, awaiting the time when he will rank them hierarchically as super- and sub-classes of each other or laterally as coordinate classes. His generalizations will begin, however, to collide and conjoin, qualifying each other or building syllogistically on each other. This increasing interrelationship corresponds to the organism's continual reintegration of differentiated functions. So, as regards individual concepts and statements, growth is toward internal complexity and external relationship. In the sense that abstraction means hierarchical integration, the child does climb the ladder as he matures, but this integration necessarily depends on a downward thrust into details, discriminations, and subclasses. He is on a two-way street: sometimes he needs to trace his over-generalizations down to their inadequate sources, and sometimes he needs to build new ideas from the ground up. He needs to place "pop fly" under "parabolic trajectory," to subordinate propositions as well as classes to each other, to derive higher abstractions from lower ones, and to utilize lower ones as instances of higher ones.

But forming concepts and making assertions concern only words, phrases, and sentences. If we follow convention in limiting our concern with abstraction to these small units of discourse, we shall not touch on what are ultimately the most important units, the wholes — the entire essay, the total story, the complete drama. Whatever their mode, let me call these whole pieces monologues, to indicate that each piece, whether spoken or written, is a sustained utterance by one speaker who is developing a subject for some purpose. In other words, *I would like to apply abstraction beyond the word, sentence, and paragraph to whole monological compositions.* Concept formation and propositional statement are very important as parts within the whole and as parts that may expand into wholes, but a curriculum sequence must be based on the growth of entire monologues such as a student would be asked to read and write, not on discrete particles.

At first, children are limited in the kinds of discourse they can produce and receive to those of lower abstraction, but as their conception matures, they add to their repertory kinds of discourse of increasingly higher abstraction. The distinction between a high abstraction level of concepts and statements, and a high abstraction level of whole pieces of speech is crucial, for a first-grader may be able to produce and understand single-utterance generalizations and syllogisms (see the earlier example supplied by the father of the parents' meeting) but be unable to write and read essays that are sustained expositions and argumentations. In other words, he begins with fragments of high abstraction embedded in a discourse of low abstraction and ends with fragments of low abstraction embedded in a discourse of high abstraction. Put another way, he learns gradually to elaborate his generalizations or syllogisms from a single utterance into the organization of an extended monologue. A sentence structure becomes an essay structure; an embedded idea, a framing idea. The elaboration and expansion of small language structures into full discourses is itself a major dimension of growth. It depends on increasing abstractive ability. To understand the importance of this point, the reader may imagine all that is entailed in shifting a generality from a sentence to a monologue.

We do have to distinguish, however, between the capacity to produce a given discourse and the capacity to receive and understand it. It seems clear to me that the reading schedule, though proceeding through the same steps as the writing schedule, and in the same order, would run ahead of the latter in most cases. That is, a student would read, say, essays of generality before attempting to write them. In fact, his own ability to monologue at that level may partly depend on prior familiarity with others' monologues at that level.

But not all discourse is monological development of a subject. Most discourse, as a matter of fact, is dialogical — conversation. Reading and writing have an oral base, which is another way of saying that monologue emerges from dialogue. And that is itself another dimension of growth. To take into account this progression from talk to print, from dialogue to monologue, I must pick up a point made at the outset — that we abstract *for* as well as *from*.

The referential relation of *I–it* must be crossed with the rhetorical relation of *I–you*, in order to produce a whole, authentic discourse. Rhetoric, or the art of acting on someone through words, is an abstractive act. That is, one performs the same activities in pitching a subject to an audience as one does in extracting that subject from raw phenomena: one selects and reorganizes traits of things, digests, codes preferentially. A course in rhetoric teaches how to present material successfully, how to find subjects; how to choose words and sentence structures, how to enchain items in sequence and patterns. Both abstracting *from* and abstracting *for* concern the same kinds of choice. The difference is whether the speaker–subject relation or the speaker–listener relation is determining the choice — the extracting from the source or the anticipation of audience response. Representing reality to oneself and presenting it to others are merely two aspects of the same process, which is abstraction. Once coding is verbal, we are hard put to conceive of it as solely abstracting from. In fact, I will make the assertion that neither abstracting from nor abstracting for exists apart from the other in the universe of discourse. "Composition" means handling both dimensions at once; a speaker always stands in some relation to both his subject and his audience. It is not always possible, in looking at a composition, to tell which choices of words and organization stemmed from selective summary of the subject and which from an effort at getting certain effects on an audience. When we think it is the latter we call the choice "rhetorical." So to delineate a sequence of kinds of discourse, we must use these two dimensions of abstracting as coordinates with which to map the universe of discourse.

Kinds of Discourse

For the sake of parsimony, the things that make for variation in discourse can be put as a matter of time and space. (1) How "large" in time and space is the speaker, the listener, the subject? (2) How great is the distance between them? (3) Do two or all of them coincide? Since these questions relate directly to the "removal" of phenomena from time and space (the degree of particularity or generality), by asking them we may easily relate "persons" (I, you, it) to levels of abstractions.

For one thing, the very activity of the discourse — thinking, speaking, informal writing, or publishing — is essentially determined by the distance in time and space between speaker and listener. If first and second persons are two parts of the same nervous system, the discourse corresponds to what we call thinking or reflecting. If they are two separate people within vocal range, the activity is speaking. If they are not in the same place, or are in the same place but at different times, the discourse will have to be in writing. Suppose now that speaker and listener are not only far apart but that instead of being a single correspondent the "listener" is plural, far-flung in space; the writing will have to be published, no mere mechanical issue, since all the substructures of the discourse will have to accommodate something common in that mass audience: vocabulary, style, allusions, logic, rhetoric will all have to gear themselves to what the average person in that audience can understand, appreciate, and respond to.

Let us array these activities in order of increasing distance between speaker and audience, between first and second person:

Reflection — Intrapersonal communication between two parts of one nervous system.

Conversation — Interpersonal communication between two people in vocal range.

Correspondence — Interpersonal communication between remote individuals or small groups with some personal knowledge of each other.

Publication — Impersonal communication to a large anonymous group extended over space and/or time.

Several features relevant to curriculum appear already. (1) The communication system expands throughout the progressions. (2) Each kind of discourse is more selective, composed, and public than those before. (3) Feedback becomes increasingly slower until it tends to disappear, which is to say that two-way transaction is yielding to one-way transmission. (4) Emphasis shifts necessarily from the communication drama between first and second persons to the bare message or content; from the *I–you* relation to the *I–it* relation.[2]

The time distance between speaker and subject at the time of speaking can usefully be represented by translating the subject into a verb tense, since tenses indicate when events happened in relation to when the speaker is speaking. With the so-called time differences, we are actually dealing with conceptual options. I may present the Civil War as *what happened* once upon a time between the North and the South, or as *what*

---

[2] These four points are very redundant, being merely different aspects of increasing abstraction; rather than pursue how it is they are factors of each other, I leave this to the interested reader.

happens whenever an agrarian aristocracy and an industrial democracy try to co-exist, or as what *was happening* when Johnny was going to college, or as what *will happen* again if we are not careful. In other words, I may symbolize the same phenomena according to different logics, which we may call time differences if we like, but which amount to different levels of abstraction.

The logic of lowest verbal abstraction is *chronologic* (narrative), because it conforms most closely to the temporal and spatial order in which phenomena occur (although already this represents considerable selecting and editing of events by our perceptual apparatus and memory, both of which have minds of their own). After playing historian, we play scientist: we assimilate a lot of narratives into a generalization by the *analogic* of class inclusion and exclusion. First I collect lots of anecdotes about Harry's behavior and then I conclude he is a bum. (I place his different acts into some class, because I see them as analogous). Or Toynbee examines what happened in several societies, classifies some events as stimuli and others as responses, and produces an historical hypothesis — at which point he is, strictly speaking, not an historian but a scientist. After playing scientist, we play mathematician: by means of *tautologic* we transform general assertions into other general assertions which mean the same thing but, because they are now in another symbolic form, imply further assertions which we could not see before. This is the level of equations and definitions. By transforming x through the tautology of an equation into y plus 3 I can now view x in a new light that permits me to infer the unknown from the known. Similarly, defining man as the glory, jest, and riddle of the world transforms an entity into a new symbolization whereby I see it differently. Thus tautologic produces *what may happen,* aspects of phenomena we could not infer merely from chronological or analogical abstractions, although without these two stages of processing the phenomena first we could not arrive at tautology.

For an example of the whole progression, imagine an on-the-spot recording of what is happening before the guillotine, then an eyewitness account of what happened one day during the French Revolution, then a historical generalization about the Reign of Terror, then a political scientist's theory about revolutions starting right and moving left.

I will now recapitulate what I have just said in the form of another progression, this time of increasing distance between first and third persons, between the speaker and his subject.

what is happening — chronologic of perceptual selectivity
what has happened
what happened — chronologic of memory selectivity
what was happening
what happens — analogic of classification
what may happen (will, could, etc.) — tautologic of transformation

What is important for a curriculum in this are: (1) Just as the logics employed lead us up the abstraction ladder, so do the human faculties successively employed — perception, memory, and ratiocination. (2) One stage cannot take place until the ones before it have taken place. (3) The phenomenal subject expands increasingly in time and space until the subject begins to become logic itself; that is, "events" become less and less space-time bound, and in being processed from narratives to generalizations to theories, an enormous amount of phenomenal material is "used up" and replaced, in assertions, by logic. Or, (4) outer events are more and more substituted for by inner events, in accordance with the definition of codification.

Doing a little tautological transforming myself:

what is happening — drama — recording
what happened — narrative — reporting
what happens — exposition — generalizing
what may happen — logical argumentation — theorizing

Thus some traditional categories of discourse — drama, narrative, exposition, and argumentation[3] — become redefined in

[3] Drama replaces description, which is not truly a distinct mode of discourse, being some kind of either narrative or general statement.

terms of (1) distance between speaker and subject; (2) levels of increasing abstraction; and (3) a sequence of activities or skills which the student should learn how to do — record, report, generalize, and theorize — in that *order* (keeping in mind that we are referring to whole discourses, not just to sentences). In learning these skills he would be also mastering chronology, analogy, and tautology.

But this speaker–subject progression considers only *what,* not *for whom.* So we now attempt to integrate it with the progression of the speaker–listener relation by imagining a speaker recording, reporting, generalizing, and theorizing at each of the four degrees of distance from his audience. Let us suppose, for example, that I am sitting in a public cafeteria eating lunch. People are arriving and departing, passing through the line, choosing tables, socializing. I am bombarded with smells of food, the sounds of chatter and clatter, the sights of the counter, the tables, the clothing, the faces, the gesticulations and bending of elbows. But I am not just an observer; I am eating and perhaps socializing as well. A lot is going on within me — the tasting and ingesting of the food, reactions to what I observe, emotions about other people. I am registering all these inner and outer stimuli. My perceptual apparatus is recording these moments of raw experience, not in words but in some code of its own that leads to words. This apparatus is somewhat unique to me in the way it selects and ignores stimuli and in the way it immediately connects them with old stimuli and previously formed conceptions. It is difficult to separate this sensory recording from the constant stream of thoughts that is going on simultaneously and parallel to the sensory record but may often depart from it. This verbal stream is the first level of discourse to be considered. The subject is *what is happening now,* and the audience is oneself.

Now, while sitting in the cafeteria I may discourse to myself at any level of abstraction: within the frame of what is happening in and around me (introspection and observation), I may embed what happened (memories triggered by ongoing stimuli), what happens (general reflections prompted by the scene), or what may or could happen (theoretical considerations also generated of the moment). Thus, self-verbalization may be about the four major *whats* of the abstractive hierarchy, but the three higher ones occur as fragments within the encompassing discourse of what is happening; indeed, memories, generalizations, and theoretical thoughts are a part of the ongoing inner action.

Suppose next that I tell the cafeteria experience to a friend some time later in conversation. For what reason am I telling him? Would I tell it differently to someone else? Would I tell it differently to the same person at another time and in different circumstances? These are not rhetorical questions but questions about rhetoric. The fact that my account is an unrehearsed, face-to-face vocalization, uttered to *this* person for *this* reason at *this* time and place and in *these* circumstances determines to an enormous degree not only the overall way in which I abstract certain features of the ongoing panorama of the cafeteria scene but also much of the way I choose words, construct sentences, and organize parts.

If in speaking to my friend I treat the events at the cafeteria as *what happened,* the subject will necessarily partake a little more of my mind and a little less of the original matter. Although the order of events will still be chronological, it is now my memory and not my perceptual apparatus that is doing the selecting. Some things will stick in my mind and some will not, and some things I will *choose* to retain or reject, depending on which features of this scene and action I wish to bring out. Of the details selected, some I will dwell upon and some I will subordinate considerably. Ideas are mixed with material from the very beginning, but the recollection of a drama — a narrative, that is — inevitably entails more introduction of ideas because this is inherent in the very process of selecting, summarizing, and emphasizing, even if the speaker refrains from commenting directly on the events.

Of course, instead of recounting the cafeteria scene to my friend in person I could write it in a letter to an audience more removed in time and space. Informal writing is usually still rather spontaneous, directed at an audience known to the writer, and reflects the transient mood and circumstances in which the writing occurs. Feedback and audience influence, however, are delayed and weakened. Written discourse must replace or compensate for the loss of vocal characteristics and all physical expressiveness of gesture, tone, and manner. Compare in turn now the changes that must occur all down the line when I write about this cafeteria experience in a discourse destined for publication and distribution to a mass, anonymous audience of present and perhaps unborn people. I cannot allude to things and ideas that only my friends know about. I must use a vocabulary, style, logic, and rhetoric that anybody in that mass audience can understand and respond to. I must name and organize what happened during those moments in the cafeteria that day in such a way that this mythical average reader can relate what I say to some primary moments of experience of his own.

But I do not have to treat the events in the cafeteria as a narrative. Whether talking to a friend, corresponding to a known group, or writing for publication to a mass readership, I may speak of my cafeteria experience as *what happens,* in which case I am now treating my once-upon-a-time interlude at the cafeteria as something that recurs. I have jumped suddenly, it seems, from narrative to generalization. Actually, as we have said, ideas creep in long before this but are hidden in the processing. Now they must be more explicit, for only by renaming the experience and comparing it with other experiences can I present it as what happens. No primary moments of experience recur. What we mean is that we as observers see similarities in different experiences. Only the human mind, capable of sorting and classifying reality, can do this. What I do, for example, is make an analogy between something in the cafeteria experience and something I singled out of a number of other experiences. I summarize a lot of little formless dramas into pointed narratives and then I put these narratives into some classes, which I and others before me have created. In this third stage of processing, then, the cafeteria scene will become a mere example, among several others, of some general state-ment such as "The food you get in restaurants is not as good as what you get at home," or "People don't like me," or "Ameri-cans do not socialize as readily with strangers in public places as Italians do," or "The arrivals and departures within a con-tinuous group create changes in excitation level comparable to the raising and lowering of electric potential in variously stimu-lated sensory receptors." It is apparent that these sample gen-eralizations could all have contained the cafeteria experience as an example but vary a great deal in their abstractness, their range of applicability, their objectivity or universal truth value, and their originality.

Finally, in its most distilled form, I might speak or write about the cafeteria experience without referring directly to it at all, even as a brief example, for I might be developing an anthropological theory in which the generalization about how Americans socialize in public places would be combined with other generalizations similarly derived from other material. The events of that scene have been so thoroughly subsumed now by my abstracting that they no longer appear as such — but they are nevertheless a part of my discourse. And again, this theory might be developed in a conversation, correspondence, or publi-cation, thereby becoming subject to the differentiating qualities of colloquial speech and formal writing, private or public monologue.

In this suggestive rather than systematic way, let me pursue the intersecting of speaker–subject and speaker–listener rela-tions, beginning with self-verbalization.

Interior Dialogue

In small children, interior dialogue is vocalized as Piaget's "egocentric speech," or prattle; in older children it goes under-ground, as designated here. Reflect for a moment on how differ-ent the qualities of style, rhetoric, allusion, tone, and organiza-tion will be when the same subjects are discoursed about in the "socialized" speech of conversation, correspondence, and formal writing. Although some people talk much as they think, still we always scan, censor, select, re-name, reorganize, etc., all this material before speaking of it to another. Intent is different (consider the rhetorics of rationalizing to oneself and of persuading another), and we take our first step toward universalizing the material and the expression of it so that our external listener may understand what we say and and be affected by it. In interior dialogue we have subjective, spontaneous, inchoate beginnings of drama (what is happening), narrative (what happened), exposition, (what happens), and argumentation (what may happen). As it bears on curriculum, this means that students would tap, successively, their inner streams of sensations, memories, and ideas, as raw material for recordings, narrative reports, and essays of generalization and theory. This cycle is both immediate and developmental: for example, older students might rewrite a subjective recording as a report to an outside audience, and younger students would not attempt to tap introspections.

Conversation

When the communication system expands from two parts of a single nervous system to two or more separate nervous systems, introspection comes out as something like, "I'm getting tired." Observation comes out as "Yond Cassius has a lean and hungry look" (which, we note, is Caesar talking to himself as much as to Antony; the progression from interior to exterior dialogue is truly gradual). Retrospection comes out as gossip, anecdotes, more or less formal reports. Generalization and argumentation may come out as a socratic dialogue of ideas, or analogy and tautology may be put in the service of emotional dialectic as generalizations and argumentations used to persuade an interlocuter.

This is the place to say that so far in this scheme I have been considering only declarative assertion; we must not forget the imperative and interrogative modes, which fill up a great deal of both dialogue and correspondence. When they prevail is when speaker and listener are proximate and known, when response and two-way transaction are possible. They disappear as feedback disappears. It is commands, entreaties, admonitions, and question-and-answer that most strongly assert the action relation of first and second persons. Catechisms and imperatives, along with retorts, make the existential, rhetorical, and behavioral features of *I–you* most keenly felt. On the other hand, the longer one person monologues uninterruptedly, the more his discourse is likely to subordinate his relation to his listener in favor of his relation to his content; that is, he is less and less influenced by the presence and responses of his interlocutor and becomes more like someone writing to someone else at a distance.

Dialogue, internal or external, will establish language as *behavior,* like any other behavior — spontaneous, ongoing, expressive, manipulative — an attempt to *do* something to or for or against or with another "party." This is the genesis of rhetoric. In succeeding kinds of discourse, emphasis will naturally shift to language as *reference to* behavior, then finally to language as *logical transformation,* meta-language.

Correspondence

Correspondence is dialogue-at-a-distance, an exchange of written monologue between parties too small to require publication of the discourse and known enough to each other so that more personal rhetoric, allusion, etc., is appropriate. The designation is meant to include any kind of writing to a small, familiar audience, whether in letter form or not. Writing must somehow compensate for the loss of voice features such as stress, pitch, and intonation, and for the loss of gesture and facial expression. Correspondence offers an excellent opportunity to teach some of the real functions of punctuation, diction, and stylistic devices. Commas, dashes, and semicolons, ironic word choice, reversal of word order often do what we do other ways in speaking face to face. Writing should be taught as an extension of speech. Nowhere is this more sensible than with punctuation. Generally, much of writing technique is a matter of simulating or replacing vocal characteristics.

Also, correspondence permits informal, vernacular practice of the four major subjects — what is happening, what happened, what happens, and what will or might happen — but still plays up the rhetorical relation or communication drama, which remains relatively intimate and therefore much more obvious than it will be later when the second person becomes anonymous, and still later when the first person "erases himself" (which of course never *really* happens). Correspondence, however, may range from the unremitting attempts to manipulate each other of the man and woman in Ring Lardner's "Some Like Them Cold" to the socratic dialogue-at-a-distance of the Holmes-Laski letters.

Public Narrative

Increasing pluralization and therefore generalization of the second person tends to enforce higher abstractions, formal writing of the sort one would publish. Beginning perhaps with personal journals, certain kinds of diaries that are addressed neither to oneself nor to another person nor yet to the world at large, we may imagine a progression of writing that is personal in the sense that it is about the speaker but that is aimed at a general audience and therefore employs the sub-structures of the language more universally. We may establish a gradient of discourse here going from accounts of personal experience recorded immediately or on successive dates, to retrospective accounts written increasingly longer after the events; in other words, from personal journals to detached autobiography. Then the emphasis shifts from *Tom about Tom* (autobiography) to *Tom about Tom and Dick(s)* (memoir) to *Tom about Dick* (biography) to *Tom about Dicks* (chronicle). First one writes about recent personal experience, then about remote personal experience, then about one's own and others' combined experiences as one recalls them, then only about the experience of other individuals, then about group experience — the latter two being of course secondhand.

A number of the implications of this spectrum need to be brought out. Enormously important for the abstractive process, when writing about one's own experience is the time interval between the events and the recording or narrating of them. Am I writing while in the same state or stage as when I underwent the experience? How much other experience that has occurred in the interval is now influencing how I tell what happened then? Writing about oneself of a long time ago is very much like writing about another person. Tom-now and Tom-then are in a very real sense two different persons (first and third.) Just as the transition from verbalizing to oneself and vocalizing to another is gradually effected, so is the transition from talking about oneself to talking about other people and things. Eyewitness accounts and memoir, in which the speaker becomes less protagonist and more observer, are steps in this transition. The key to memoir and eyewitness accounts is *resonance* between the main figure or figures (the third person) and the observer-narrator. Why does he choose to tell this? The answer is that he responds personally to what happened, and includes these responses in the narrative; he identifies, he treats that other *as if* it were himself — just as he treated his former self as if he were another.

If the main issue in recording and reporting one's own experience is time distance, the main issue in writing of others' experience is often space distance. Is the writer there where the events occurred? How does he know what he claims to know? Channels of information become now a great concern. They are essentially three for a reporter close enough in time and space to the principals to have first-hand information. Knowledge of what happened externally he knows by virtue of being an *eyewitness;* knowledge of the inner life by virtue of being a *confidant*; and knowledge of background and general circumstances by virtue of being a member of a special *chorus* or limited community in which the principals circulate and are known. Note that the three channels of information are increasingly abstract: what I can know as eyewitness comes from my perceptual recording of sights, deeds and words; what I can know of others' inner life is their verbal abstraction of it for me; what I can know of background and general circumstances is by definition summary, secondhand generalizations and inference. Now, a narrator playing all three roles is able to give most immediate and complete coverage. In fiction, the narrator opts to play two or three of these roles in varying ratios; in actual reportage, the narrator can only play certain roles in certain ratios. If, say, he has observed the subject but not interviewed him, he cannot report inner life except by inference. The more remote and tenuous the relation in actual life between the narrator and his people, the more he must fall back on chorus information; and the more remote the people and events are in time and space, the larger and vaguer the chorus and the more its information is in the form of written documents, until finally we are consulting reference libraries for all we will ever know about historical personages and events. But these communal documents are what? Well, they are precisely the kinds of discourse we have been discussing before — recorded conversation, letters, journals, autobiographies, memoirs, chronicles, previous histories. So our student writing and reading his way through this spectrum is learning to be a case-writer and historiographer.

He is also learning to be a naturalist. I have neglected for some time now the reporting of non-human phenomena, which began with the subjective sensory recording of interior monologue. The nomenclature for narratives of nature is harder to come by. You will have to imagine their equivalents at various stages of the spectrum — accounts of what is happening and what happened among some animals, plants or stars. I assume a scientist does a lot of writing up of field trips, lab experiments, etc., before he sits down to analogize particular events into an hypothesis about "recurring" or "repeatable" events. Of course he is limited to two roles at the outset — eyewitness and chorus. Alas, he cannot play confidant to animals and plants. He has the same essential problem, however, as his brethren in the humanities: how to tell the observer from the observed, the symbolizer from the symbolized, the information from the informer.

Public Generalization and Inference

Increasing extension of the subject over time and space, and increasing distance between speaker and the original phenomena which he is abstracting about, makes for a gradual transition between the chronologic of reporting what happened to the analogic of generalizing what happens, all by a process of summaries of summaries of summaries. The logic of classes has of course been at work long before this frontier is crossed, but working *implicitly*. Now, in generalization, it becomes more the subject itself and is dealt with explicitly in lead paragraphs and lead sentences as well as in the choice of frankly classificatory nouns. The tense shifts to the present tense of generalization.

Regardless of whether the discourse is about people or things, if it purports to tell what happens (rather than what happened) it is scientific. Science and history are distinguished from each other not so much by what they are about (sociology and psychology are scientific, and geology and evolution are historical) as by the level of symbolization to which phemonema have been abstracted. But what about generalization that did not take off from empirical phenomena in the first place? Precisely, a student who has abstracted from the ground up will automatically know the immediate difference between science and metaphysics — that one creates classifications inductively by sorting narratives and records of empirical data, and the other inherits — *a priori* — its classes and categories. In short, whereas science has worked its way, so to speak, through all the kinds of discourse up to this level, metaphysics *begins* here. Ultimately, of course, the difference between the two is not so great and the student should discover this too. *A priori* categories are inherited from somewhere; their provenance from the evidence of the senses is simply much less direct and evident than with science, which, for its part, rests ultimately too on assumptions, the assumptions built into that very neural apparatus which must do all the symbolic processing and about which science knows yet so little.

In these upper reaches of the spectrum, rhetoric becomes increasingly synonymous with formal, explicit logic. That is, the classes the speaker creates and the inferences he makes on the basis of them constitute his main way of appealing to and acting on his reader. Since formal logic is such by communal agreement, rhetoric becomes as impersonal as it can get, in keeping with the growing anonymity of the speaker. As a loose rule, we may state that the pluralization and generalization of one "person" tends to bring on the pluralization and generalization of the others.

Of course chronology, analogy, and tautology are frequently found in mixture; discourses combine narrative, expository generalization, and inferential argumentation. For the student, however, it may be helpful to assign readings and writings in a purer form first, so that in mixing them he will know what he is doing and so that he will recognize the mixture in others' writing. At a fairly concrete level, for example, a biology textbook, a government manual on procedures, Montaigne's essay on friendship, and Pope's *Essay on Man* represent sustained generalization. At a higher level, *Summa Theologica, A Critique of Reason,* and *Language, Truth, and Logic* represent sustained logical combining of some prior generalizations assumed as premises. But many an argumentation of a theory contains not only the generalizations from which it derives, but also, embedded in the generalizations, some bits of narrative as illustration or documentation of the generalizations (Einstein's *Relativity* is an example). In fact, most high-order discourses contain, like parentheses within parentheses, successive embeddings of the lower orders which they have subsumed.

Eventually "English" passes into symbolic or mathematical logic, à la Russell, Quine and others. This is where the two subjects can be integrated to form a continuum from raw phenomena to the abstractest symbolizations. I think I have already indicated how the more substantive subjects of history and the sciences could be integrated, and at which levels. Literature tends to fall along the lower ranges, with drama as the point of departure, fiction coinciding with the range of "personal history" that precedes communal history, and poetry playing the whole scale. It is interesting that poetry cannot be located by abstraction and person. To distinguish it from other discourse we have to invoke a different concept altogether — Suzanne Langer's division between discursive symbols and presentational

tion. Only a model of one or two dimensions more could justly represent the simultaneous play of both relations and the many wheels within wheels. I will try to indicate some of this multidimensionality a little more than I already have, because it is what would make the schema more realistic.

In either inchoate or vestigial form, something of every level is found at every other level. The major movement of drama-narrative-exposition-argumentation is contained already in interior dialogue — in streams of perception, memory, and ratiocination. Likewise, the three main logics — chronology, analogy, and tautology — operate at every level. Fragments of generalization and theory, for example, are embedded in narrative as single utterances and embodied in narrative as implicit classes and propositions upon which selection and emphasis are based. Although these three logics have a phase where each emerges fully as the dominant organization, each also appears in the others as a germ or vestige. Conversation and correspondence can be monologuist narrative and exposition as well as dramatic interplay. Biography may contain all of the discourses that precede it, either en bloc or assimilated — dialogue, letters, diaries, and first-person documents by the subject himself. In general, the spectrum begins by featuring rhetoric and secreting logic within it; it ends by featuring logic and looking barefacedly unrhetorical, but anyone who has climbed the abstraction ladder knows how much the rhetoric of history, science, and metaphysics is merely buried in the previous processing.

None of this theory, however, deals explicitly with one extremely important dimension of growth. What about the mythic mode of representation? The schema just presented is based on the hierarchic symbolizing of actualities, on information-processing. But people fictionalize. They project into invented stories those unobjectified forces of the psychic life that are hard to name or even recognize. Storying is a mode of abstracting, allowed for in the foregoing theory but not actually treated there. At any time of life we have some inner material that we cannot express directly and explicitly; we have to say it indirectly and often unconsciously, through metaphorical fiction.

Usually, the older we grow the more we can objectify and talk explicitly about feelings and ideas, but a child must for a long time talk and read about these things through a sort of allegory. There are two reasons for this. One is that he is not ready to acknowledge to himself a lot of his thoughts and feelings because he must defend against them. Another is that his abstractive powers are not developed enough to enable him to conceptualize, name, and interrelate these intangible things. As regards their deepest inner material, adults are in the same boat, and so we have art. In other words, students progressively push back the frontier of the unknown by converting the implicit into the explicit, but no one can go all the way.

Whereas adults differentiate their thought into specialized kinds of discourse such as narrative, generalization and theory, children must for a long time make narrative do for all. They utter themselves almost entirely through stories — real or invented — and they apprehend what others say through story. The young learner, that is, does not talk and read explicitly about categories and theories of experience; he talks and reads about characters, events, and settings. For children, though, these characters, events, and settings, are charged with symbolic meaning because they are tokens standing for unconscious classes and postulations of experience, the sort we can infer from regularities in their behavior. The good and bad fairies are categories of experience, and the triumph of the good fairy is a reassuring generalization about overcoming danger. In the *Wizard of Oz* the wizard is a humbug and the bad fairy can be destroyed by water; Dorothy is stronger than she thought, and the adults are weaker than they appear at first. *Alice in Wonderland* is amazingly similar in statement. A tremendous amount of thought — and intricate, at that — underrides these plots. Objects, personages, and settings are categories of experience; actions are relations among the categories; and plot is a kind of syllogism or postulation — all of which is to say again that children must represent in one mode of discourse — the narrative level of abstraction — several kinds of conception that in the adult world would be variously represented at several levels of abstraction. Growth, then, is toward a differentiation of kinds of discourse to match the differentiation in abstraction levels of thought. Myth, legend, fairy tale, and fiction only appear to be a low level of discourse like narrative reportage; actually they are a compression of several levels into one, which accounts for their multiple layers of meaning.

Growth in the fictive mode runs somewhat the reverse of the abstractive order I have been describing. Whereas the symbolizing of recognizable, objectified experience does, I believe, proceed up the ladder from the here-now to the there-then, it is in the nature of disguised psychic material that one symbolizes it first in the there-then and only gradually comes to represent it in explicitly personal terms. In other words, as regards his external observation and his acknowledged feelings, a child moves, in his speaking and writing, from the firsthand, first-person concrete levels of abstraction toward the secondhand, third-person timeless realms of abstraction. But as regards his unconscious psychic life, he moves along a continuum that begins in the far-fetched, with things remote from him in time and space, and works backward toward himself. As children we project ourselves first into animals, fantastic creatures, folk heroes, and legendary figures. Slowly, the bell tolls us back to our sole self. Gradually we withdraw projection as we become willing to recognize the personal meaning symbolized in our myths, and able to objectify inner experience to the point of treating it explicitly.

One can question whether this seeing through our own fictions and fantasy is really a good thing, since the original function of such symbols, obviously answering a profound need, is destroyed by such rational lucidity. The contemporary trend, for example, to scientize mythic literature by abstracting archetypes out of the stories and translating their figures and actions into explicit categories and statements of experience, converts this literature from a mode which serves a psychic function into a common declarative mode having other functions. The same is often true of critics' expository essays interpreting the symbols and "hidden meanings" of poetry and fiction. It is interesting that authors and children are aligned in their antagonism to this analytical process of de-symbolizing, perhaps because it breaks the unconscious psychic engagement with the symbols that is the point of the creations in the first place. The fact is that as people grow up, they tend to withdraw projections anyway, to become lucid realists who see through symbols. Is there any point in hastening this de-mythologizing by talking in class about archetypes and by chasing down literary symbols?

There is a way, however, in which a theory of literature such as Northrop Frye's can help the teacher in describing the growth of his students along the fictive dimension. I have in mind especially his five kinds of heroes — the supernatural or divine figure, the mortal but miraculous man, the king or exceptional leader, the average man, and the ironic anti-hero. This progressive scaling down of the hero not only traces the history of literature, with its shifts in dominant literary modes from epic and myth to legend and romance, to tragedy, to bourgeois novel and play, to a very inner and underground fiction, but it also corresponds to what I have been calling the withdrawal of projection or the movement from the far-fetched there-then to the actual here-now. Every child recapitulates the history of the species to this extent: he first embodies his wishes for power in fantasies of omnipotence akin to the myths and epics of divine and supernatural heroes; the figures, actions, and settings he likes to read about and create are as remote as possible from himself and the circumstances of his own life. Starting at this extreme, he shrinks his fantasies increasingly toward figures like himself dwelling in his own time and place, thus passing through legend and romance, tragedy, and realistic fiction. This passage comes about partly because he is gaining real power as he grows up and consequently needs less and less to fantasize about power, and partly because he is becoming more aware of and explicit about his wishes and fears and thus wants to read and write about them for what they are. All this, however, does not mean that in the beginning he cannot already appreciate familiar realism in some conscious areas of experience, or that later, he will not still need the far-fetched modes for unconscious areas of experience.

Any sort of fiction is as much an abstraction of reality as any other mode of discourse — and a high level one at that. The concrete aspect of story is misleading because, as I have implied, it actually compresses the logic of classes and the logic of propositions into a chronological mode. What psychoanalytic theorists have called "condensation" in the primary-process thinking of dreams is, I feel sure, just this compression of three logics into one: concrete figures, objects, and settings are doubling as classes of experience; concrete actions as the relations among classes; and plots as syllogisms. Hence so much rich ambiguity and potent symbolism. Stories have a "logic of the events" and reach a "conclusion." Obviously, it would make no sense to blandly place fictive stories on the same rung of the abstraction ladder as narrative reportage of actualities just because they both follow a chronological order, for the previous assimilation of experience underlining each is different. The story of Odysseus or of Beowulf, for example, is actually very abstract in the sense that it condenses the experience of a whole culture as much as, though not in the same mode as, obviously more abstract books such as today's sociological treatises. Like earlier man, the child cannot read and write psychology and sociology, but he can handle these subjects through ambiguous concrete symbols that, in effect, but not in appearance, span several stages ahead in the abstractive hierarchy.[4] A piece of narrative reportage too, however, may span upward in the same way, as with the case history, where the personages and their behavior are clearly offered as representative of a type of person and a type of behavior. Indeed, typological narratives, including a lot of biography and history, are one of the transitional ways that one order of abstraction becomes a higher order. Thus a stu-

[4] The thesis of Claude Lévi-Strauss's *The Savage Mind* is that primitive people do not think less, or less intricately, than civilized adults; they merely think in a different mode.

dent might, like case writers and novelists, say in effect *what happens* by telling *what happened.* Narrative becomes generalization gradually, by embodying ideas in representative peoples and actions (as in Orwell's "Shooting an Elephant"), and by embedding generalities in the text of the story to "point" it (as in fables with morals).

But what about a sequence of specific linguistic structures and rhetorical issues? Shouldn't these be serially focused on one at a time? I think this naturally happens as one reads and writes his way through some kind of progression like the one sketched here. That is, the various abstraction levels of discourse — recording, reporting, generalizing, and theorizing — and the varieties of audience relationships, automatically program, if you will, a meaningful series of linguistic structures and rhetorical issues. This can only be an hypothesis of course, but I think that shifting, say, from narrative discourse to that of explicit generalization necessarily entails shifts in language and rhetoric and thus tends to bring successively to the fore different language structures and compositional issues. Tense, as I have indicated, is one thing that changes. But so do other things. Adverbial phrases and clauses of time, place, and manner that abound in recording and reporting give way, in generalization and theory, to phrases and clauses of qualification; temporal connectives, transitions, and organization perforce yield to logical ones. The kinds of paragraph structure one tends to use shift. And generally, the increasing complexities of sentence structure, described as embeddings by transformational grammar, accompany the increasing cognitive ability to interrelate and subordinate classes and propositions. What will further the normal growth of sentence elaboration is practice in language tasks that are at bottom intellectual. The point is that a specially devised program of isolating these structures and issues for the student is unnecessary and probably misguided, since those very things will arise in developmental succession anyway if the correspondence I am claiming between levels of discourse and stages of growth is true.

Qualifications about Sequence

This whole theory of discourse is essentially an hallucination. Heaven forbid that it should be translated directly into syllabi and packages of serial textbooks. I say this for two reasons. The first is that the theory is far too schematic to be true. I know from research I have conducted in grades 4–12 that the development of writing is unbelievably relative, to the point that pupil capacity seems to vary as much horizontally throughout a population of one grade as it does vertically through the grades. The second reason is that we would know a lot more now about growth in reading and writing if textbooks had not prevented teachers from actually finding out these facts about sequence that the textbooks were guessing at (but advertising as scientific truth). The main source of knowledge about children's language development could be the classroom itself. In an open, trial-and-error approach, pooling experience and utilizing a tentative theoretical framework, teachers could amass specific information about what children can and cannot read and write at various stages of their growth.

This approach was the method of the research in writing I alluded to above, in which a number of teachers in different schools participated, trying out assignments I had devised, and talking over the results with me every week or so. I read a huge number of the papers produced and analyzed them qualitatively (i.e. unscientifically) in all sorts of ways. The theoretical framework was essentially the one I have been developing here. One of my rare privileges was to be able to examine side by side what children of very different ages did with the same assignments.

Here are some conclusions I drew. Among the many non-developmental factors that cloud the issue, the past conditioning of the students (and of the teachers) accounts for more variation than anything else. To separate out developmental differences is virtually impossible when white middle-class fourth-graders write rings around the ninth-grade ghetto children in sensory and memory writing, and when eighth-graders of one suburb handle eye-witness nature reportage better than tenth-graders of a similar suburb. An assignment to invent an interior monologue, which we didn't dare try out below the ninth grade, was unwittingly fulfilled very well by some fourth-graders doing a fiction assignment. At every turn of the road we ran into the disconcerting fact that what a student could write seemed to depend more on his out-of-school language environment and previous school training than on his age. It is true, however, that certain assignments were not given below a certain grade because the teachers did not want to inflict a debacle on either the children or themselves. Certain upper cutoff points on the abstraction ladder seemed obvious for certain ages. And only a few teachers of very able twelfth-graders would even consider assigning an essay that argued a theory from premises, a refusal that was undoubtedly based on good judgment but that may show the ineffectuality of present schooling rather than a developmental limit.

But the question is not just what students *can* do but what they *want* to do and *how* they do it. Fourth- and fifth-graders, we found, could perfectly well take sensory notes of ongoing events and write them up, or write streams of memories and compose one of them into a narrative. But they preferred the latter because, as I interpret, memories come out of themselves — are personal and already meaningfully organized — whereas sensory recording is relatively impersonal and hard to organize. But, if the children are taking observational notes on the behavior of pets and intend to put these notes to use afterwards for practical purposes, then the recording assignment again becomes personal and meaningful, and they want to do it. Older students can record at a random locale and *give* the recording meaning, starting merely with an observer's curiosity that is not enough for younger students. Elementary school children can write monologues of various sorts but are more at home with dialogues, which follow a familiar and dramatic social give-and-take and don't require the logical continuities of monologue. The monologues they write most easily are stories, of course, which follow a chronological continuity. But they do not make up stories easily without stimulants and prompters, and when they do, the stories are seldom original. Abandoning stereotypes — creating original classes and vehicles — does seem to be a feature of growth. If asked actually to create, not paraphrase, an essay of generalization, they simply make it so short that the real issue of continuity does not arise. So although one could claim that they can write high-level discourses of generalization, and even theory, this would be true only of utterances so brief as to finesse the basic assumption underlying my whole analysis of discourse — that the linguistic capacity to sustain such monologues depends on a cognitive capacity to explicitly interrelate classes and propositions, and to embed lower-order abstractions, as samples or evidence, into higher orders. Whether they are writing stories or ideas, children over-condense at first, and only later become able to elaborate and expand. But many underdeveloped junior and senior high school students have the same limitations: they write only synopses, and one can feel their reluctance to leave the haven of narrative.[5]

As for reading, it may well be that abstractive limitations hit children more in connection with individual concepts and statements than with total continuity, since all a reader has to do is *follow* the organization. But if he cannot comprehend the concepts and statements, he is lost. It seems to me that elementary school children are *able* to read many levels of discourse if the embedded terms are relatively concrete, but it is also true that many younger children are simply less *motivated* to read exposition than they are stories. I suggest, therefore, that curriculum experimenters look for abstractive problems in comprehension at the level of concepts, but look for them in composition at the level of the whole monologue.

[5] In *A Student-Centered Language Arts Curriculum, Grades K-13: A Handbook for Teachers* (Boston: Houghton Mifflin Company, 1968), I have reported more fully many of the experiments referred to here and have attempted to describe sequences of assignments in English consonant with the theoretical stand taken in this essay.

Towards a Summary

In trying to summarize discursive growth, I find that two current formulations — one by Piaget and one by Basil Bernstein — can encompass many of the dimensions considered here. Like most comprehensive and valuable theories, Piaget's notion that people decenter from an initial egocentricity as they get older is probably not susceptible of final empirical proof. And yet everywhere I look I see evidence. A few days ago my first-grade daughter, who was lining up some miniature bowling pins for me to shoot at, set up the wedge so that it pointed to herself, not to me. I see examples in missing commas, poor transitions, "faulty" logic, lack of focus, incoherence, anti-climax, and a host of traditional compositional problems. Rather remarkably, the theory of egocentricity relates to both abstracting from and abstracting for. This is perhaps because some *consciousness* of abstracting must precede growth in either. Differentiating among modes of discourse, registers of speech, kinds of audiences is essentially a matter of decentering, of seeing alternatives, of standing in others' shoes, of knowing that one has a private or local point of view and knowledge structure. Thus the following list of continuities is merely a set of variations on the theme of decentering.

1. From the implicit, embodied idea to the explicitly formulated idea.
2. From addressing the small, known audience like oneself to addressing a distant, unknown, and different audience.
3. From talking about present objects and actions to talking about things past and potential.
4. From projecting emotion into the there-then to focusing it in the here-now.
5. From stereotyping to originality, from groupism to individuality (this seems paradoxical, but egocentrism, as Piaget says, is basically just centrism, whether ethnocentric, geocentric, or heliocentric; it is regorging received ideas without critical *detachment*).

At this point Piaget's theory overlaps, it seems to me, with Bernstein's theory of restricted and elaborated codes. This theory, I hasten to say, is intended to describe social class differences in the use of language, not developmental differences, but the restricted code of the lower class and the elaborated code of the middle class constitute a dimension remarkably parallel to general growth irrespective of class. Speaking of the middle class, Bernstein says, ". . . speech becomes an object of special perceptual activity . . . The speaker is able to make highly individual selections and permutations. The language facilitates the verbal elaboration of subjective intent, sensitivity to the implications of separateness and difference and points to the possibilities inherent in a complex conceptual hierarchy for the organization of experience." All this contrasts with the code of the lower-class speaker, which "progressively orients him to descriptive rather than analytical concepts."[6]

The code differences run along the same line as the developmental shifts we have discussed: implicit to explicit, ethnocentric to individualistic, increasing choice, increasing abstractness of conception, increasing consciousness of abstracting (speech being an object of special perceptual activity), increasing elaboration. Furthermore, valuable correlations seem to exist between Bernstein's formulations, which are currently being submitted to further investigation by other researchers, and the theories of cognitive style specialists like Jerome Kagan, Herman Witkin, and R. Gardner. Kagan has hypothesized a dimension of impulsive to reflective; Witkin, a dimension of global thinking to analytical thinking and of field-dependent perception to field-independent perception; Gardner, a dimension of leveling to sharpening (non-discriminating to discriminating).[7] Whether

[6] These quotations were culled from two articles of Bernstein, "Social Class and Linguistic Development: A Theory of Social Learning" and "Social Class, Linguistic Code, and Grammatical Elements" and quoted in an unpublished paper, "Social Class, Language and Cognitive Behavior" of a doctoral student at Harvard, Anita Rui, to whom I am indebted for the correlations between Bernstein's work and that of the cognitive style specialists referred to below.

[7] The latter two are important dimensions in Heinz Werner's theory of cognitive growth (*Comparative Psychology of Mental Development*).

from child development or not, any such research-based theories about verbal and cognitive variation are helpful in thinking about curriculum continuity. Bernstein's general hypothesis that forms of social control govern language codes leads to formulations that are especially suggestive when one considers how much the language of disadvantaged students seems to be arrested at a stage that middle-class children go easily beyond. Thus we have fourth-graders writing rings around ninth-graders because the latter's development is constrained by the forms of social controls in their environment. Since I came across Bernstein only after drafting the theory of discourse developed in this essay, I was fascinated to find such statements by him as this: ". . . a shift from narrative or description to reflection — from the simple ordering of experience to abstracting from experience — also may signal a shift from we-centered to individual experience."[8]

The primary dimension of growth seems to be a movement from the center of the self outward. Or perhaps it is more accurate to say that the self enlarges, assimilating the world to itself and accommodating itself to the world, as Piaget puts it. The detailed forms which this movement takes are various and often paradoxical. In moving outward from himself, the child becomes more himself. The teacher's art is to move with this movement, a subtle act possible only if he shifts his gaze from the subject to the learner, for the subject is in the learner.

[8] "Linguistic Codes, Hesitation Phenomena and Intelligence." *Language and Speech*, Vol. 5, Part I (January–March, 1962), 12.

CHAPTER THREE

Drama: What Is Happening

This chapter magnifies that range of the abstractive spectrum referred to earlier as *what is happening* and relates it to self-verbalization and vocalization. I would like to argue here that drama and speech are central to a language curriculum, not peripheral. They are base and essence, not specialties. I see

Reprinted with permission of the National Council of Teachers of English from *Drama: What Is Happening* (Champaign, Ill.: NCTE, 1967). I am very grateful to the following people for criticizing the manuscript for me: Courtney Cazden and Anita Rui of Harvard University; Elizabeth Cawein of Weeks Junior High School in Newton, Massachusetts; my fellow members of the Study Group in Drama of the Anglo-American Seminar in the Teaching of English (Dartmouth, 1966) — Douglas Barnes of the University of Leeds, Anthony Adams of the Crutchfield Comprehensive School, West Bromwich, England, and Benjamin DeMott of Amherst; and NCTE consultant readers Arthur Eastman of the University of Michigan and Alfred Grommon of Stanford.

For criticism of the section of this paper employing concepts from transformational grammar ("Dialogue"), I am much indebted to Wayne O'Neil of Harvard, Edward Klima of M.I.T., and John Mellon of Harvard. They are not to be held responsible, however, for my presentation and use of these concepts.

drama as the matrix of all language activities, subsuming speech and engendering the varieties of writing and reading. But to regard it so is to reconceive it, to perceive in it the germinal ideas and actions of other language behavior.

In order to exploit for pedagogical purposes some similarities between theatrical and everyday drama, I am going to set shuttling some two-way metaphors between them. That is, I will speak broadly and use ambiguously both the word *drama* and some other terms that name its components. For the sake of possible stimulus value, I hope the reader will indulge my shifting reference without always explicitly signaling the shifts. My purpose is to make art and actuality illuminate each other. Some definite recommendations for teaching methods will follow this theoretical discussion.

Stage Drama and Street Drama

The script of a play is a transcription of what a spectator should see and hear. The spectator is a kind of sound camera who records the play, but because he is human, he records it in a discursive way. If his sensory recording were written down — the vocal sounds as dialogue and the rest as stage directions — it would roughly recapitulate the script (except for Shavian extravagances).

This same spectator could go out of the theater into the street, note down his sensations as he witnessed some action, and thereby create a script of his own. Drama does not have to be vocal, or even human; it might be a dumb show or a game among dogs. Drama is any raw phenomena as they are first being converted to information by some observer.

Although the action that takes place in a theater has been premeditated, it has fundamentally the same impact on the spectator as real-life events. True, *knowing* that the events are artifactual, not actual, gives the spectator a different mental set and alters somewhat his responses, but in viewing both, the spectator is coding events directly for himself; he is looking on, not hearing about. What we witness both onstage and outside comes to us unmeditated by any other mind, unabstracted except by our own perceptual apparatus, undigested, unreported. One reason an author works in the dramatic medium is that he wants the deeds he has invented to hit us at the same "gut" level that actualities do.

A comparison with narrative may help. The action of a narrative is not ongoing, it *has* gone on; it is *reported* action. As such it is a résumé of some previous drama — summarized and abstracted *by somebody,* a reporter, narrator. Although grammar tells us that the difference between *what is happening* and *what happened* is a time difference, much more than time is involved. Tense is a relation of speaker to events: if the events are unrolling before his eyes — ongoing — they are being coded for the first time by someone who is *attending* them (or "assisting at" them, as the French say) and who is therefore in the same plane of reality as the act-ors. This is his point of view. His coding of events is a first-order abstraction. As a report of what happened, narrative is a second-order abstraction. Compare the sensory stream of someone watching a football game with the Sunday newspaper account of the same game. Narrative is a further abstraction of some observer's prior abstraction. What makes events past is reporting them. What makes events present is attending them. Whereas narrative summarizes drama, drama elaborates narrative. Consider a reviewer's recapitulation of a play performance, then a dramatization of a short story. Whether actual or artifactual, drama is *what is happening,* with all that this implies.

A play of course only pretends to be raw, unabstracted phenomena; actually it is a highly sophisticated conceptual creation. Characters, settings, words, and deeds are carefully selected and patterned. In fact, one essential difference between the theater and the street is this difference between order and randomness — which is another measure of abstraction. So in this sense a play is very abstract. Characters tend to be representative, the actions symbolic, the words and deeds significant. By selecting and shaping, the artist abstracts reality into forms that mean something to the audience. The impact of a play is dependent on some resonance between what is happening on stage and what has happened in the life of the spectator. No matter how far he is from being a king or from killing someone, the beholder of a revenge tragedy finds, for the feelings of betrayal and the murderous desire for quittance, some analogs in himself. The playwright invites generalization but does not generalize himself because he does not speak. In presenting what is happening he is implicitly saying what happens. This transferability is what we mean when we speak of the significance of a work.

Nevertheless, a play is not a novel, poem, biography, or essay. Despite its selectivity, conceptualization, and implicit generalization, it is an imitation of physical action and therefore still shows characteristics of the unabstracted phenomena it imitates; it is calculated to affect a spectator in much the same way a real-life drama does when he is confronted with it. And you don't have to know how to read to follow a play. You can't backtrack, because words and deeds move irreversibly in time. Reflection is held to a minimum, to "thinking on your feet," though of course you may reflect later in tranquillity as you do about real events. No guiding voice conducts you, plays host, summarizes and explains. (To offset this lack of interpreter, some playwrights may create a character who serves as a narrator or as a *raisonneur,* but note that to the extent such a character remains a *character,* and the play a drama, the result is merely to create a new level of unabstracted information.) Regardless of how cerebral a statement some character may utter, it is the behavioral utterance of the statement and not its content that makes a play dramatic. If the author wanted his audience to reflect more en route, or wanted to reflect for them, he would write in another form.

Drama is the most accessible form of literature for young and uneducated people. It is made up of action; and the verbal action is of a sort we all practice all the time. A kindergarten child or an older illiterate can soliloquize and converse, verbalize to himself and vocalize to others. No written symbols are required. Drama is primitive: not only does it hit us at the level of sensation, affect, and conditioned response, but it seems in all cultures to be virtually the first, if not the first, verbal art to come into being, because it is oral and behavioral and functional, evolving directly out of real-life activities, such as propitiating gods, making rain, and girding for war. Indeed, a number of modern trends, such as happenings and the anti-play, have exerted force to return drama to a communal actuality.

The components of a play may be divided into the verbal and nonverbal. What the spectator sees, or what he hears that is not vocal, is of course contained in the stage directions. These are objects and actions that might be referred to in speech, and indeed are often referred to by the speakers. But speech, though on the one hand merely another recordable action, is obviously a very special one because it is symbolic. Not only can it be referred to like other objects and actions, but it refers in turn to other things not perceptible to an observer — things offstage, inside the speakers, and on invisible levels of abstraction. The speech components of a play are *soliloquy, dialogue,* and *monologue* — addressing oneself, exchanging with others, and holding forth to others. The nature of each of these, and the relations among them, imply some very important things, I believe, for the teaching of discourse. I would like to examine each of these three speech components as phenomena of both the theater and real life.

Soliloquy

Though theatrical convention and necessity require that a soliloquy be voiced, it is supposed to be unuttered thoughts, self-verbalization. Soliloquizing is thinking. At least as early as Henri Bergson and William James, psychologists have suggested that thought is inner speech. The notion has been subscribed to since by the social psychologist George Herbert Mead and by an impressive roster of contemporary specialists in learning theory and child development that includes Piaget, Vygotsky, Luria, and Bruner. The general concept is that most of our thinking, the verbal part, is a kind of unvoiced conversation within oneself. After acquiring speech socially, through interaction with other people, the child begins to distinguish between the speech he utters for himself and the speech he utters for others. At first he voices aloud all speech, typically failing, in his egocentricity, to discriminate talking to himself and talking to another. Once he does discriminate, this early "egocentric speech" splits into internal and external discourse. Both are instrumental but have different functions: internal speech serves to process information as a guide to action; external speech serves to communicate. The earlier egocentric speech is a "thinking out loud," a running accompaniment to play and thus probably not distinguished by the child from his other bodily actions. Part of this patter is simply a verbal encoding of physical things, and part is planning and self-direction — all of which he later inhibits because it is not socially adaptive, and may even be socially detrimental if uttered aloud. In shunting some of his own speech underground, the child is in effect internalizing the words, forms, and ideas of other people, since he learned them by imitation and interaction (although it is probable that he acts on this material according to innate structures he was born with). Anyone can observe for himself some of the stages of this internalization. A child will tell himself aloud in perhaps his parents' exact words that "we should not touch the vase." Children thinking about a task can be seen to move their lips, so that an experienced lipreader can tell what they are thinking as they verbally mediate the task.

It is not generally acknowledged just how much the social medium of exchange and the chief instrument of thought are one and the same — language. Outer and inner speech reciprocally determine each other; they are a serpent with its tail in its mouth. What needs emphasis, however, is the probability that thought is the internalization of social processes. For this emphasis I turn to George Herbert Mead.

> In reflective intelligence one thinks to act, and to act solely so that this action remains a part of a social process. Thinking becomes preparatory to social action. The very process of thinking is, of course, simply an inner conversation that goes on, but it is a conversation of gestures which in its completion implies the expression of that which one thinks to an audi-

ence. One separates the significance of what he is saying to others from the actual speech and gets it ready before saying it. He thinks it out and perhaps writes it in the form of a book; but it is still a part of social intercourse in which one is addressing other persons and at the same time addressing one's self, and in which one controls the address to other persons by the response made to one's own gesture. That the person should be responding to himself is necessary to the self, and it is this sort of social conduct which provides behavior within which that self appears. I know of no other form of behavior than the linguistic in which the individual is an object to himself, and, so far as I can see, the individual is not a self in the reflective sense unless he is an object to himself. It is this fact that gives a critical importance to communication, since this is a type of behavior in which the individual does so respond to himself.

. . . .

The unity and structure of the complete self reflects the unity and structure of the social process as a whole; and each of the elementary selves of which it is composed reflects the unity and structure of one of the various aspects of that process in which the individual is implicated. In other words, the various elementary selves which constitute, or are organized into, a complete self are the various aspects of the structure of that complete self answering to the various aspects of the structure of the social process as a whole; the structure of the complete self is thus a reflection of the complete social process. The organization and unification of a social group is identical with the organization and unification of any one of the selves arising within the social process in which that group is engaged or which it is carrying on.

The phenomenon of dissociation of personality is caused by a breaking up of the complete, unitary self into the component selves of which it is composed, and which respectively correspond to different aspects of the social process in which the person is involved, and within which his complete or unitary self has arisen; these aspects being the different social groups to which he belongs within that process.[1]

[1] George Herbert Mead, "Self" in *On Social Psychology: Selected Papers,* ed. Anselm Strauss (Chicago: University of Chicago Press, 1964), pp. 206, 208.

If I understand Mead correctly, self and mind are social artifacts, and the constituents of the self mirror the constituents of society; thought involves incorporating the roles and attitudes of others and addressing oneself internally as one would address another externally.

As inner conflict becomes more important in the plays of Shakespeare, the soliloquies become longer and more numerous. Compare those of Brutus and Hamlet. Reflected in Hamlet's soliloquies are various "voices" of his culture, society, class, and family — belief systems, attitudes, points of view, and roles. These could be personified and each assigned certain lines from his soliloquies, thus creating an external dialogue to prove Mead's point. Hamlet is full of voices, ghosts. So is Willy Loman. And so are we all. Consider what it means when we say "I keep telling myself . . . ," "I debated with myself . . . ," "I talked myself into . . . ," and so on. Biologically each of us is a whole; only cognitively and culturally can we be split into speaker and listener.

To consider the same issue in reversal, the whole of a play may be considered as a soliloquy by the playwright, who is ventriloquizing. A playwright says what he has to say not through a monologue but through a colloquy of created voices. The ensemble of these voices externalizes his mind. This kind of ventriloquizing amounts to fractionating the total voice production of which he is capable, to breaking down his self into the many points of view, attitudes, and roles which actually and potentially comprise it. The failure of young readers to appreciate Dickens' caricatures, and the failure of critics to "understand" *Waiting for Godot,* stems from an insistence that each character be a whole person instead of recognizing that the dramatis personae are a whole person and that the characters are embodied tendencies and potentialities of that person. Becket's Gogo and Didi, Pozzo and Lucky are components of personality, paired. If a play works, communicates, it is because the same social forces that have installed voices in the author have also installed them in the spectator. Whether the playwright is sociological like Shaw, psychological like Strindberg, or both like Arthur Miller, their characters tend to speak as both personality components and as social forces. In *After the Fall* Miller finally completed a technical innovation begun by O'Neill in *Emperor Jones,* Tennessee Williams in *The Glass Menagerie,* and himself in *Death of a Salesman;* by exploiting the incorporation process for the very form of his play, he made the stage a peopled head.

To place the discourse of the individual in a perspective that helps us to contemplate it most usefully, let us imagine a set of concentric circles (see figure) that has the individual as

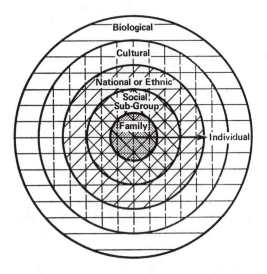

Concentric Contexts Determining the Individual's Language

center. Each circle is a determining context for the smaller circles it contains, and therefore it governs them. "Larger" means "more universal." The largest or most universal context is the biological; that is, the structure of our nervous system is what admits of the least individual variation, and the characterization of more localized contexts will be some more or less direct translation of man's biological being. If something innate explains language acquisition, as linguists of Noam Chomsky's persuasion believe, it is governed by this context. My own persuasion is that the predispositions for uniquely human kinds of abstraction are indeed innate, but not as "ideas," as Chomsky would have it. "Language universals," logical structures found in all languages, are probably reflections of neural structures as suggested by Warren McCulloch, for example.[2]

The next largest circle is the culture, which determines the thought of the individual through belief systems and postulates about nature built into its languages and supporting institutions. Within this context lie the cognitive differences among, say, Indo-European, Chinese, Eskimo, and Hopi cultures such as Benjamin Lee Whorf talked about. Though much disputed, Whorf's hypothesis that the categories and grammar of a particular culture shape the thought of the individual is bound to be *relatively* true. What is an open issue is the proportionate influence on the individual of language universals on the one hand and cultural idiosyncrasies on the other — the relative weight of the innate and the acquired.

But this issue is complicated tremendously by the influence of the successively smaller contexts — the national and ethnic society, social subgroups, and the family. Undoubtedly influenced by Basil Bernstein's hypothesis that forms of local social controls dictate one's linguistic code, researchers are increasingly inclined to see connections between "cognitive styles," language styles, and life styles. A mother's way of talking to her child influences the child's cast of thought, but the mother's way of talking is in turn governed by her class and ethnic heritage. If schools wish to influence how students think and speak, they must take account of all the language contexts which have determined how the individual already thinks and speaks, then create a new language community that will induce what is missing. The head of any soliloquizer is peopled — long before he comes to school.

Although we customarily regard thought as private and internal, it is in many respects really very impersonal and external.

[2] *Embodiments of Mind* (Cambridge: Massachusetts Institute of Technology Press, 1965).

Original permutations of thought may be very individualistic, but the tool of thought is an instrument socially forged from biological givens. The abstractive structures we are born with are open and flexible and may, as research in anthropology and cognitive styles show, produce very different abstractions in different groups. It is from his groups that the individual learns these *particular* ways of cognizing and verbalizing. In view of this, a pedagogy based on provoking or eliciting thought presupposes that a child is already capable of generating the required kinds of thoughts. Asking "stimulating" questions and assigning "stimulating" reading invites the student to put out but does not give him anything, as teachers of the disadvantaged know well. In order to generate some kinds of thoughts, a student must have *previously* internalized some discursive operations that will enable him to activate his native abstracting apparatus. Furthermore, it may be possible to tap inner speech too soon.

Elicitation has a place certainly at some stage of instruction, but more basic is to create the kinds of social discourse that when internalized become the kinds of cognitive instruments called for by later tasks. The failure of disadvantaged students to think and talk middle-class prose stems obviously from their not having been talked to and with in the way middle-class people talk to and with their children. But even the most advantaged child will never escape the cognitive limitations of family, class, social role, etc., unless the school provides him a kind of discursive experience to internalize that is different from what he has internalized at home. The cranium is the globe, but the globe *any* child grows up in is always too small for later purposes, especially in the chameleon civilization we know and are increasingly going to know.

Among the considerations that impel me to agree essentially with Mead, even though he seems to slight innate factors, is that his theory jibes with other important theories. When Erik Ericson relates kinds of societies to kinds of ego structures, he too is assuming that an individual is a walking model of his social world. Freud's concept of superego — the voice of conscience — is based on the notion of introjecting outside attitudes. And cognitive growth, according to Piaget, depends on expanding perspective by incorporating initially alien points of view. This "decentering" is the principal corrective to egocentrism (and ethnocentrism, geocentrism, etc.).

All this is to say that soliloquy is more than a stage device. It is really a colloquy among one's cultural, social, and familial voices. All the wickedly intricate relations of thought and speech, mind and society, heredity and environment are involved in it. As we participate in and observe the daily dramas of life, we are constantly soliloquizing at one or another level of abstraction, depending on where our attention is centered at the moment. If we are lying in bed late at night beside an inert husband, like Molly Bloom, we may dwell on memories and related feelings and reflections. We may fantasy, like Walter Mitty, in defiance of active surroundings. Or fasten hypnotically on immediate sights and sounds like Macbeth in the dagger scene. Or, like Hamlet, mix a debate on one's own fate (itself rather general) with a contemplation of man's fate (*very* general).

Whatever the abstraction level of the soliloquy, the action of soliloquizing is itself ongoing behavior, the drama of what is happening inside someone. *Speaking and writing are essentially just editing and abstracting some version of what at some moment one is thinking.* In asking a student to write something, the teacher is in effect asking him to take dictation from some soliloquy he will be having under the influence of the assignment conditions. Thus seen, the conditions of the assignment may appear in a new light. The different kinds of writing we recognize as descriptive, narrative, and reflective depend on the abstraction level of the soliloquy, which in turn depends on the soliloquizer's present attentional focus. However influenced by outside constraints, such as assignment conditions, any soliloquy is spontaneous — one does not at a given moment choose what is to come up for editing. Therefore — and this is the main point — what becomes available for someone to put on paper when he is writing has already been greatly determined by prior verbal experience. Reading is a very potent source of contents and forms which a student stores and may later utilize in soliloquy. But I am going to claim that conversational dialogue exerts the most powerful and direct influence on the content and forms of soliloquy. That is, interaction is a more important learning process than imitation, whatever the age of the learner.

Dialogue

Real-life conversation is primary discourse — spontaneous, ongoing, unpondered, and uncomposed. The dialogue of a play purports to be such. In a word, dialogue is *extemporized*. It is generated of the moment and moves in time, governed by setting and circumstances as well as by the wills of the speakers. Neither speaker knows what he is going to say a minute hence because that depends on what his interlocuter says in the meantime and perhaps also on what is going on around them. Face to face, each relies on nonverbal cues from voice, face, and body, as well as on the lexical meanings of the words. Feedback is fast, clearing up or aggravating misunderstanding. I call this "primary" because (1) it is the first discourse we learn; (2) it is the least abstract in the sense of least planned and ordered, however abstract individual words and statements may be; and (3) it is discourse in its most physical and behavioral form. That is, face-to-face dialogue is most localized in time and space. It blends with and depends on other physical action, both of the body and of surroundings. It relies on the interlocuters' seeing and hearing each other, on such things as ostensive communication (pointing). It is often interchangeable with other action; a kiss or a blow can replace words and vice versa. Organization by one mind is minimal, for interaction partly determines the selection and arrangement of words, ideas, and images. Continuity, topic — and even word choice and sentence structure — are governed in large measure by the social transaction.

One of the unique qualities of dialogue is that the interlocuters build on each other's sentence constructions. A conversation is verbal collaboration. Each party borrows words and phrases and structures from the other, recombines them, adds to them, and elaborates them. An exchange may consist of several kinds of operations, or rather, co-operations, such as question-answer, parry-thrust, and statement-emendation, demonstrated most powerfully in the theater by stichomythia (the rapid alternation of speakers).

Inseparable from this verbal collaboration is the accompanying cognitive collaboration. A conversation is dia-logical — a meeting and fusion of minds even if speakers disagree. Of course much conversation is not ideational but consists of ceremonial formulas, admonitions, commands, and exhortations. But where thinking is involved at all, it is joint thinking; dual *logos* is at work. While participating in this mental duet, we are incorporating the points of view, attitudes, ideas, and modifications of ideas of our partner, even if we openly reject them.

I would like to advance an hypothesis that dialogue is the major means of developing thought and language, and to illustrate the kinds of co-operations responsible for this development.

Evidence of various sorts suggests to me that two general limitations characterize the thought and speech of younger children and of older but "disadvantaged" people — the failure to *specify* and the failure to *relate,* both of which I will subsume under the concept of *qualifying.* Specifying is an act of analysis; relating, an act of synthesis. The verbally immature or disadvantaged student needs, on the one hand, to discriminate and specify more, which would move him toward details; and, on the other, he needs to connect in, for example, temporal, causal, and contrastive ways, and to subordinate ideas to establish rank and salience, all of which would move him toward higher abstraction. Like an embryo, he needs, paradoxically, to grow simultaneously in opposite directions, toward differentiation and integration — to elaborate specialized parts within the whole, and to interrelate parts throughout the whole.

Linguistically, qualifying works out as the expansion of sentences. The undeveloped person tends to overcodify and say simply, "I saw a fight yesterday," begging a hundred questions. Or, if he does specify, to string the bits of information out into a mere list, a sequence of kernel sentences or simple clauses joined with *and* that orders and juxtaposes items in a neutral and coordinate fashion: *Yesterday I went to the playground. Two guys were fighting. I never saw them before. They were wearing black jackets and one kicked the other and there was blood . . .* , and so on. In this latter case not only is economy sacrificed (a different but important matter) but salience and focus are missing: is the speaker's "point" or center of interest the strangeness of the fighters, the violence, or what? And lack of relatedness creates ambiguity: did the kick draw blood, or did both fighters bear blood from earlier blows?

To take specifying alone for a moment — it consists not just of finding precise nouns and verbs but of modifying the nouns with adjectives, appositives, prepositional phrases, participial phrases, and relative clauses; and similarly, of modifying the verbs with adverbs, prepositional phrases, and relative clauses indicating time, place, manner, and so on. All these elements elaborate a sentence, of course, but the information in most of these modifiers *could* be predicated in separate sentences, which, as I have said, is just what the undeveloped person tends to do first, a tendency parodied by Dick and Jane: *I see a ball. The ball is blue. It is in the grass. I saw it yesterday.* The last three sentences add to the first sentence three more facts about the ball and the speaker. This satisfies half of our requirement for qualification — specifying — but at this point all we have is enumeration of facts, a meaningless inventory. Such a sequence might be rhetorically calculated to get the gradual dawning effect of recognizing the ball, and this is indeed a fine justification for using kernels. Seldom is this the case, however, with naive speakers or basal readers (the dullness of the latter owing, precisely, to their meaningless inventories, as well as to their use of structures that trail by several years the child's development).

To fulfill the other condition of qualification — logical relation — the four kernels might be synthesized into: "I see in the grass the blue ball I saw yesterday." Is the information the same as before? Yes, and no. We have the same four facts, but syntax has generated new information beyond any of the isolated facts, namely the main point of the whole experience, that the ball seen today and the ball seen yesterday are one and the same. The new information is of a higher order than the old information: it is about the speaker's verbal intent; it tells us what he considers salient and what is merely supportive data. Though the pronoun *it* linguistically relates the ball of today and the ball of yesterday, this intersentence connection does not suffice to synthesize the data of the four-sentence sequence, whereas the syntax of the new sentence renders the whole meaning residing in the speaker's intent. (Note that in fusing the four sentences into one I had to change the article from *a* to *the* and shift the order of *in the grass* to avoid ambiguity, the first being a semantic adjustment logically entailed by the relative clause, and the second a practical adjustment to offset one of the hazards of complexity.)

But suppose the speaker's experience was something else. Suppose when he saw the ball the day before he thought it was green: "This ball in the grass I saw yesterday is *blue*." Or the ball has changed location, from sidewalk to grass: "This blue ball I saw yesterday is now in the grass." Syntax speaks; implicitly, it conveys the more abstract, less palpable information of larger meanings. As Basil Bernstein has theorized, the undeveloped speaker assumes rather than renders his verbal intent.[3]

Except for those relatively rare cases where the accumulation of kernels best conveys our experience or idea through an inductive rhetoric that forces the reader to do the relating, it is clear, I think, that expanding kernels and other simple sentences is a necessity of mature thought and speech. Specifying alone remains a dubious blessing, mere addition, until the powerful calculus of syntax interrelates items to form logical wholes.

What are the resources of syntax that do this? They are several, but the chief ones are *conjoining* and *embedding*.[4] Two sentences might be connected by one of the coordinating or

---

[3] "Linguistic Codes, Hesitation Phenomena and Intelligence," *Language and Speech*, 5, Part I (January–March 1962), 31–46.

[4] Some transformational theorists may construe subordinate conjoining as a subclass of embedding, but for my purposes here it will be clearer to treat them as different operations.

subordinating conjunctions, all of which except *and* are interpretive — *if, or, although, while, unless,* and so on. Or one potentially independent sentence might be embedded in another as a noun clause, relative clause, participal phrase, infinitival or gerundive nominalization, appositive, or absolute; even such noun modifiers as adjectives and prepositional phrases represent embeddings of reduced sentences. (A kernel is defined, in one way, as containing no embeddings or conjoinings.) Conjoining tends to relate items explicitly (with words that declare the relation, conjunctions). An example is: "Since they were starting another game, he decided to return later." Embedding relates implicitly (by substitution and insertion alone). An example is: "Seeing another game about to begin, he decided to return later." Although these two are the chief tools for achieving logical relation through syntax, there are others, including correlative constructions ("the more . . . the more," "not only . . . but also") and sheer juxtaposition as regards the placement of movable elements (governed by transformation rules).

I think of this critical relation between qualifying thought and elaborating sentence structures as having two levels. At the first level items are specified only; at the second, in addition to being specified, they are also related. The first level can be attained, in a single kernel, only through predicate adjectives and through certain adverbial phrases that are not embeddings; or in a sequence of kernels, through the stringing of discrete predications. Only at the second level, however, where conjoining and embedding relate these kernels can such specificity reach fruition and become true qualification. A *single kernel sentence* asserts an unqualified or barely qualified statement and thus establishes the minimum for level one. A *kernel with non-embedded modification* fulfills level one in some measure but cannot specify much without succeeding sentences. A *sequence of kernels with nonembedded modification* will in most cases still fall short of level two also, because "nonembedded modification" excludes not only noun and relative clauses but also nominalizations, participial phrases, appositives, and adjectives and prepositional phrases modifying a noun. That is, only at level two do the full syntactic resources get put into play.

By way of doing a little qualifying myself — without, I hope, introducing too much intricacy — I should add that some sentences containing references to other sentences may remain linguistically simple while actually achieving cognitive complexity. Thus: *I like that.* (When *that* refers to a whole preceding idea). Or *In that case we should buy tickets now.* (*In that case* referring probably to a previous clause, often an *if*-clause.) Or *They disagreed nevertheless.* (*Nevertheless* acting as an inter-sentence connector). Since such referencing merely entails pronouns, adverbs, and adverbial phrases, it may not technically change the status of a kernel sentence, and yet it is clear that a previously predicated idea is being either incorporated into the kernel or joined to it. *In effect,* a sort of indirect embedding or conjoining has taken place, discernible at the semantic but not the linguistic level. Transformational theory has not yet dealt much with such referencing, but I would regard these sentences as a separate class of simple sentences equivalent to some more complex sentences, since this kind of referencing is just the sort of logical relating achieved by the syntax of more complex sentences. I would argue, however, that not all referencing has the same power to relate. *It,* referring to a one-word antecedent, and *however,* referring to a whole clause, stand in the same power proportion as a true kernel sentence does to a sentence containing embedding or conjoining.

The point of this analysis has been to establish a parallel between qualifying thought and elaborating sentence structures. I have treated the expansion of kernels only because the operations involved in it apply at all levels of complexity, not because the educational problem is merely one of getting beyond kernels, which most children can do in *some* measure very early. But a good linguistic education would insure that, as a student worked cognitively downward toward detail and upward toward generality, he would be helped to find, or to activate, the matching language structures. There is no virtue in complexity for its own sake but only for the sake of this matching. The only reason for encouraging a student to elaborate his sentence structures, aside from stylistic variation and rhetorical effect, is to enable him to qualify his information and communication. The less facility one has with conjoining and embedding, the more one's thought is likely to remain crude. Again, discourse does not just convey thought, it also forges it.

I think the classroom method for helping students learn to qualify thought and elaborate sentence structures should be essentially the same method by which children spontaneously learn to do these things out of school. Although direct imitation is part of the method, it is probably not the main part or the most effective; very young children will join two clauses with *because* because they have heard such sentences but may fail to establish any true causal connection. I would like to submit that the most important and successful way we learn linguistic forms is by internalizing the whole give and take of conversations. That is, the learner synthesizes what *both* A and B said, especially when he himself is one of the interlocutors, and produces in the future a new sentence that is a conjoining, embedding, or other synthesis of the two utterances. (This "future sentence" would of course not necessarily be about the same content; I am speaking of the *structural* synthesis informing the content.) Whatever the form of synthesis, he produces a more elaborate statement than was either before. This is a very different process from the learner's hearing an utterance of a certain construction one time and then at another time, in what he perceives to be a similar situation, constructing a similar sentence. This is imitation and is undoubtedly of value in acquiring language and shaping thought, but as in the causal construction, the learner is often wrong. Furthermore, although extensive reading and listening prepare for elaboration, they do not seem to activate it. Imitating one utterance, finally, is not as potent a method as synthesizing two utterances.

Let's look now at some of the possible operations or transactions comprising dialogue that could teach elaboration of thought and speech. One such operation may be question-and-answer. A makes a statement and B asks for more information. The answer to B's question may be a sentence or a potential sentence which if fused with A's original statement would result in a conjoining, an embedding, or some simpler expansion. At the same time, the original statement is qualified by the further information or different point of view.

A: I saw the dog again.   I saw that dog again *down*
B: Where?   *along the river.*
A: Down along the river.

    (Verb modification with a locative phrase.)

A: I saw that dog again.   I saw that *shaggy* dog again
B: Which one?   *that we found in the barn*
A: That shaggy one we   *yesterday.*
    found in the barn
    yesterday.

    (Embedding — adjective and relative clause.)

A: The bill will never pass.   The bill will never pass *be-*
B: Why not?   *cause it's too close to elections.*
A: It's too close to elections.

    (Subordinate conjoining — causal.)

A: The bill will never pass.   The bill can't pass *until after*
B: Never?   *elections.*
A: Well, I mean it can't
    until after elections.

    (Subordinate conjoining — temporal.)

A: I just talked with   I just talked with Mr. Ana-
    Mr. Anaheim.   heim, *the assistant director of*
B: Who's he?   *the program.*
A: The assistant director
    of the program.

    (Embedding — appositive.)

In the following operation B directly embeds A's utterance:

A: He won't talk to them.
B: Whether he talks to them or not makes no difference.
        (Embedding — noun clause.)

A: Who's going to help him get out of that mess?
B: His getting out of that mess is no business of ours.
        (Embedding — gerundive nominalization.)

B may incorporate or annex the main idea of A's utterance by referring to it, but may not directly embed the utterance. Needing to refer and not wishing to repeat, B finds a linguistic structure accommodating both A's idea and his own overlying idea.

A: Who's going to help him get out of that mess?
B: That's not our business.
        or
    Regardless of his mess, we have to go ahead.
A: I think the price is too high for them.
B: They'll pay despite the price (whatever the price) (nevertheless.)

Another operation consists simply of appending a qualifying clause to the original statement:

A: He'll make it, don't worry.   He'll make it *if he finds the*
B: If he finds the key in time.   *key in time.*
      (Subordinate conjoining — conditional.)

A: These angles will always   These angles will always be
    be equal, then.   equal *so long as these lines*
B: So long as these lines are   *are parallel.*
    parallel.
      (Correlative conjoining.)

Perhaps the most important operation occurs when B adds to A's statement another fact, point of view, or argument that (he implies) A should allow for. The conjunctive or embedding relation between the two statements is only implied in the conversation but would be supplied by A in a future discourse:

A: Government ownership of railroads would not work in the U. S.

B: It has worked in England and France.

Although government ownership of railroads has worked in England and France, it would not work in the U. S.

(Subordinate conjoining — concessive.)

or

The fact that government ownership of railroads has worked in England and France does not mean it will work in the U. S.

(Embedding — noun clause.)

A: Miss Leary scowls all the time and makes you stand outside the door.

B: I've heard that she gives the lowest grades in the whole school.

Miss Leary scowls all the time, makes you stand outside the door, and gives the lowest grades in the whole school.

(Coordinate conjoining — additive.)

or

Miss Leary not only scowls all the time and makes you stand outside the door, she also gives the lowest grades in school.

(Correlative conjoining.)

A: King Alfred voluntarily abdicated.

B: But that was after the assembly had already stripped him of his power.

Already stripped of his power by the assembly, King Alfred voluntarily abdicated.

(Embedding — participial phrase.)

These examples are crude compared to the dynamics of continuous dialogue, where this process of questioning, appending, and amending may continue across many utterances, and sometimes with A further elaborating B's contributions. Also, the reader will have to extrapolate from these examples to more complicated dialogues involving multiple speakers.

The qualifying of thought and elaborating of sentence structures develop together. Outside the classroom this development through vocal exchange occurs all the time, but in the classroom it can be furthered deliberately by creating kinds of dialogue in which questioning, collaborating, qualifying, and calling for qualification, are habitual give-and-take operations. Adjustive feedback by no means requires an adult always, but an adult may be necessary to establish the necessary characteristics of the conversation. If interlocutors do not really engage with each other, pick up cues, and respond directly, or if they merely listen out the other and wait for their turn to speak, nothing very educational will happen.

I am asking the reader to associate dialogue with dialectic. The internal conversation we call thinking recapitulates previous utterances *as amended and expatiated on.* The social actions underlying vocal exchange have counterparts in the forms of language. Dialogical structures and linguistic structures can be translated into each other. Thus what *can* seem like dead, academic matters in a classroom are drama-tizable.

This is easiest to see with conjoining, because conjunctions are explicit. Additives represent agreement; adversatives, contradiction; concessives, provisos, and conditionals, a degree of acceptance and a degree of resistance. (More naive students tend toward additive and adversative operations only — the full agreement of *and* or full disagreement of *but* — and need to have other possibilities demonstrated for them.) Constructions of time, place, and manner are born of when, where, and how questions motivated by the listener's desire to get more information from his speaker. The true *because* is born of *why.* The creation of relative clauses and the insertion of interpretive "signal words" like *however, moreover,* and *therefore* stem from a felt need to relate statements for the benefit of the listener. The way the speaker becomes aware of this need is through questions of clarification or other feedback indicating that the listener does not understand the relations among items or statements in the utterance.

Although a student might come to use connectors, expand modifiers, subordinate clauses, and embed sentences just by sheer imprinting — stylistic imitation — I think it is safe to say that such learning would never go far or deep without the functional need for qualification and elaboration arising in dialogue. This is why I do not think exercises with dummy sentences, no matter how superior the grammar, will teach students how to use various linguistic constructions appropriately and habitually. The expatiation process of dialogue adjusts a speaker's verbal and cognitive instruments at just the moment when he cares most and in just the way that he, individually, needs this adjustment.

Monologue

The first movement away from dialogue is monologue, by which I mean the sustained, connected speech of the sort the term designates in the theater. It is the opposite of stichomythia, which represents dramatic crest, the high point of fast verbal interaction when interlocutors shoot single sentences or half sentences at each other in rapid alternation. Notoriously, monologue risks breaking a play, because the longer one speaker holds forth, the more the content of his speech overshadows his interaction with other players. Most television scenarists make it a point of never letting a character utter more than two or three sentences at a time.

Whatever prompts a monologuist to talk so long carries with it some continuity or organizing principle that is likely to take the audience out of the present. If the monologue is a report of what happened, it goes into the past; if a generality about what happens, it goes into a timeless realm. Besides chronological and logical continuities, a third possibility exists — a sequence ordered by some psychologic — but such a monologue approaches soliloquy again and, indeed, is usually played by the actor with a certain self-absorption as a kind of musing. In all cases, monologue tends to carry us away from the existential circumstances of its utterance and to lessen interaction with a listener, but the psychological sequence remains more dramatic than the chronological or logical because, like a soliloquy, it has the present dynamic of moment-to-moment inner movement. The great success of Jerry's monologues in *The Zoo Story* is due to the fact that his stories and generalizations are themselves strongly enchained by a psychologic stemming from his intention to break Peter open and reach him, to find out if continuing to live is worth it.

Monologue is the bridge from drama to other forms of discourse. It is the beginning of a speech less moored to circumstance and audience, that floats more freely in time and space. It moves closer to organization and composition, because *some single mind is developing a subject.* It is the external pathway to writing. And yet, ultimately, every monologue has some dialogue for its context, from which it issues. This is true whether the monologue is an anecdote in a back porch gossip session, the Greek messenger's report of Hippolytus' death, or a novel. Lest the third example seem out of order, let me suggest that any written composition may be usefully deemed a monologue, since it is uttered entirely by one person, and that the dialogue from which it issues is simply more extended over time and space. The solo work we call a novel is part of a slow-moving, long-range dialogue-at-a-distance between the novelist and his society. Feedback comes in the form of public response, sales, reviews, and critical articles.

Among monologues, then, the critical distinction is between the face-to-face vocalizations, which are extemporaneous and very sensitive to audience presence and to circumstances of utterance, and written monologues, which are planned and composed in relative detachment from audience and circumstances. Further, among written monologues themselves there are degrees of composedness and detachment, in conformity with the spectrum of discourse outlined in the last chapter.

If the teacher imagines a continuum going from the one extreme of stichomythia to the other extreme of the polished solo publication, he has then an instrument of pedagogical value. For the gradations of the continuum are steps in a natural evolution from dialogue to written composition. A cumulative learning sequence can be based on these gradations that will lead the student from conversation to vocal monologue to casual writing to formal writing. (As I have indicated, a simultaneous development toward writing derives from soliloquy by an internal route.) But the first step toward writing is made when a speaker takes over a conversation and sustains some subject alone. He has started to create a solo discourse that while intended to communicate to others is less collaborative, less prompted, and less corrected by feedback than dialogue. He bears more of the responsibility for effective communication. He has moved away from drama toward narrative, exposition, and theory — the domains of writing. He has started to enchain his utterances according to some logic. The cues for his next line are not what his interlocutor said but what he himself just said. Like a jazz solo, a monologue grows by self-stimulation.

When ongoing social behavior no longer structures the discourse, some internal behavior, some logic, takes over and determines the order and arrangement of utterances. Even such one-way action as admonition, exhortation, and command cannot be sustained unless some logic is resorted to and some "argument" set in motion. To abandon the transaction of dialogue for the transmission of monologue is to drop interrogative and imperative modes and to work solely in the declarative mode. The more independent the monologue is from listener and situation, the more it becomes statement.

What enchains the consecutive declarations of the monologuist is some fusion of logical connections and rhetorical ploys. For example, chronological order might be disarranged to put an arresting event first, or the conclusion of a syllogistic argument might be placed either first or last depending on the effect desired. What is characteristic of monologue, however, and not of dialogue is the unfolding of a subject according to the logic and rhetoric of one mind. The types of monological continuity range from the "then . . . then" of chronology to the "if . . . then" of formal argument.

In another way monologue evolves from dialogue. This evolution concerns the embedding of one kind of discourse within another. The brief utterances of a dialogue may be of all sorts — a bit of description, a one- or two-sentence story, a general proposition, or an if-then syllogism. Each such utterance is a miniature monologue. The form of predication is the seed of a whole monological structure. A past tense verb, say, with modifiers of time and place foreshadows the full story predicated likewise in narrative form but allotting several sentences to one action and perhaps whole paragraphs or even longer sections to establishing time and place. The difference of course is, again, elaboration. Similarly, the one-sentence proposition or syllogism is the seed of an utterance that, if extended and elaborated, resembles what we call an exposition or argumentation. A sizable slice of conversation usually contains, embedded in it here and there, fragments of all these modes of discourse which can be developed into monologues and thence into compositions. In fact, a child can, in brief utterances, handle any of these modes, for he has the linguistic structures necessary to describe, narrate, frame a generality, and (unless badly disadvantaged) employ the if-then construction. What, precisely, he does not characteristically do is extend and elaborate these utterances beyond a sentence or two (clearly he does so sooner with description and narration) — that is, order utterances into a continuity that translates the small-unit structure of the sentence into the large-unit structure of a monologue.

A good English teacher would help the student, of whatever age, to take wing and extend one of these embodied bits of narrative or exposition. A younger student would be encouraged to sally forth from amidst a dialogue. The older student might within one class period traverse on a small scale the whole continuum of dialogue → vocal monologue → written monologue that I mentioned before as a curriculum sequence.[5] That is, he converses in a small group, extends one of his utterances before the entire class, then takes the monologue to paper and finishes it there, thus moving through a short version of the general learning progression. Because they are both mono-logical, whatever the degree of improvisation or composition, any vocal holding forth contains the same possibilities for various kinds of continuity as any written holding forth.

To ask a student to write is to ask him to make all the adjustments between dialogue and monologue that I have been describing. I am saying that a curriculum should afford the student a rich experience in not only the right kinds of conversation but also in the variety of vocal and written monologues that bridge into full-fledged public composition. The most critical adjustment one makes is to relinquish collaborative discourse, with its reciprocal prompting and cognitive co-operation, and to go it alone. The first going it alone can be simply an extended utterance within a conversation. A very important issue of psychological independence is involved. Failing to achieve this independence is a major reason why so many students — even adolescents — who can converse for hours claim they have "nothing to say" when asked to write.

Also, forsaking the interrogative and imperative modes for declaration eliminates a lot of discourse that a child is most familiar with. Add to this the well-known fact that an enormous amount of conversation is social communion, establishing and maintaining solidarity, and has little to do with developing a subject, which in fact is sometimes a pretty indifferent matter. Add further that having to develop a real subject, alone, means employing one or more of the monological orders of statement. Where does the student find such things? Only in himself of course. And how do they get there? They get there through internalization of previous dialogues. . . .

[5] For this suggestion I am indebted to Douglas Barnes of the University of Leeds.

Monologue derives from past dialogue via the internal route of soliloquy, and derives from present dialogue by soloing out of ensembles. When anyone verbalizes solo fashion, whether silently to himself, aloud to another, or on paper to the world, he must draw on discourse he has heard, had, and read. A student can give to the world only some permutations of what he got from the world. Lest this seem to slight the powers of the individual, let me add, perhaps paradoxically, that the more speech of other people one takes in, the more original will be his permutations and the freer will he be of any limited set of voices. Liberation is a matter of hearing out the world.

In summary, drama is the matrix of discourse. As information, it is the inner speech of the observer at the moment of coding raw phenomena. The corresponding educational activity is recording. As communication, it is the social speech of the participant at the moment of vocalizing face to face. The corresponding educational activity is oral extemporizing. Soliloquy is intrapersonal dialogue, which is verbal thought. Conversation is interpersonal dialogue, which is vocal speech. These two activities feed each other: when we communicate we internalize conversation that will influence how we code information in soliloquy; how we inform ourselves in soliloquy will influence what we communicate in conversation.

Teaching Methods

Let me turn now to the actual teaching methods that relate to these considerations of drama. Most of these methods have been tried at the elementary or secondary level in some public and private schools. The appropriate classroom activities may be roughly divided into active discoursing by the student — conversing and writing — and the receptive occupations such as listening, reading, and beholding. But it is in the nature of dramatic methods that this division should not hold well, for what is output for one student is often input for another. In fact, all of these activities would be woven in and out of each other.

Because it is primary, I will begin with face-to-face vocalization, which breaks down into four activities — dramatic improvisation, discussion, play performing, and monologuing. These are closely related and one can grow out of others.

Dramatic Improvisation

An improvisation is spur-of-the-moment invention of action. But this invention is done within some framework of givens or stipulations. Indeed, younger children seem to need more givens, whereas experienced improvisers can start with a bare suggestion or minimal situation. The givens may at first be props, puppets, or bits of costume that stipulate place (grocery store), personage (Smoky the Bear), or role (king). Later, these stipulations may be made abstractly: A is a parent, B a child, and B is making an excuse of some kind — an assignment of situation and relationship — or, very abstractly, A wants B to stay and C wants him to go — an assignment of a certain triadic dynamic.

By contrast with the extreme openness of the last situation, where the actors have to supply personalities, relationships, and circumstances, a very restricted form of improvisation is the enacting of stories the students have read or been told. Since, as I have said, drama elaborates narrative, what happens in this case is that the actors fill in the details of body movement and dialogue. Though it may be helpful to distinguish between *invention* and *enactment,* these two forms are only relative since the actors are always working within the constraints of some set of givens. In general, younger and less experienced children want to do roles and stories already familiar and only gradually abandon stereotypes and conventions for more original creation.

The method shifts somewhat with the age and dramatic experience of the students, but in general everybody is participating simultaneously without an audience — either in several small groups or as one class group. The story or situation to be improvised is usually discussed first. It may be a familiar domestic situation, a bit of history or social studies material, or a piece of literature. Different groups might work on the same "scene" or consecutive "scenes." Roles are rotated (no type casting) and different versions done until the potentialities of the situation have been well explored, or, of the story, well elaborated and extended. If a group wants to repeat its improvisation before the rest of the class, fine, but the goal is not performance, and the teacher does not push toward it. At a very advanced stage, however, the class may become a kind of drama workshop in which the sub-groups expect to improvise before the others so that everything can be discussed — the dynamics, the content, the roles and styles, the acting.

In fact, a powerful side effect of improvisation is the dialogue *about* the improvisation generated before, during, and after. Such conversation concerns both the task itself and ideas embodied in the material. That is, the whole class, or the sub-groups, discuss the choices of material, differences in various versions of it, consequent differences in interpretations, and hence ideas, perceptions, and values. Task-oriented or problem-centered talk turns naturally onto psychological, moral, and literary issues. Or conversely, a discussion taking off from a different point, such as direct considerations of psychological and moral issues or difficulties with a piece of literature, can turn toward improvisations for exemplification and clarification. Improvisation should be thought of as a learning process that can be exploited for many discursive purposes.

One of these is specifically literary. Before a child can enjoy drama in script form — play reading — he can do so by creating the imitative actions of which scripts are a blueprint. Later, his power to bring a script alive in his mind is constantly recharged by his continued experience in inventing dramas. For narrative, improvisation renders a special service: it translates *what happened back* to *what is happening.* For younger children this brings back to present actuality — alive — the abstraction of a story they read silently on the page or had read aloud to them. For older students, converting narrative to drama demonstrates the relationship of the two: plays specify what narrative summarizes, and narrative, unlike drama, is told by someone addressing us.

Furthermore, many fairy tales, legends, myths, and histories are extremely condensed and often told very impersonally. They lack physical detail, dialogue, and the personal points of view of either the characters or the narrator — all things that make a story more interesting and more like familiar fiction. Improvisation allows students to imagine and fill in these physical details and dialogue and, through invented soliloquies, also the thoughts and feelings of the characters. Difficulties of text, too, can yield to the process of being "cast in other terms," the existential terms of drama. And, finally, improvisation can be used as an entrée into a literary work soon to be read: the teacher abstracts key situations — say, Cassius' efforts to persuade Brutus to join the conspiracy — and assigns this as a situation to improvise before students read the work, so that when they do read it they already have an understanding of what is happening and of how differently the characters *might* have behaved. This kind of prelude also involves students more with the text.

There are several, more fundamental purposes of dramatic improvisation. Begun at an early uninhibited age, extemporizing of this sort can head off later self-consciousness, make verbalization easy and natural, increase presence of mind, and develop inventiveness. But this is only a basic discursive facility, a loosening of tongue and limbering of wit. More specific goals are to foster the ability to (1) listen closely and react directly to an interlocutor, (2) devise *ad hoc* rhetorical ploys for getting certain effects and results, (3) simulate the language, style, voice, and manner of someone of a certain type or role, (4) shift roles, attitudes, and points of view — stand in others' shoes, (5) feel from the inside the dynamics that make up a theatrical scene, and (6) act out and express real feelings in a situation made safe by the pretense that "I am being someone else."

Discussion

Discussion is another kind of oral improvisation but one especially intended to exploit the inherent relation between dialogue and dialectic. It is a dramatic method of developing intellectual powers. The main purpose is to promote the social art of conversing, the intellectual art of qualifying, and the linguistic art of elaborating. The right kind of dialogue will teach so-called exposition and argumentation better than years of premature belaboring on paper. The characteristics, listed above, that improvisation is designed to develop should transfer readily to discussion because the context is the same — face-to-face vocalization — and so is the process — feeding back and expatiating.

Differences are of degree: in discussion, body movement is minimized and the givens — topics — are simply stipulated so abstractly (by comparison) that concrete "scenes" become examples to allude to rather than to act out (although at any point in a discussion a group might resort to improvisation). And whereas improvisations *embody* ideas and issues, discussions deal with them explicitly and only verbally. It is possible, however, to shade gradually between improvisation and discussion. If the participants of a drama begin to talk directly about the issues their acts involve, or to invoke concepts, as in talky plays, then the drama shifts toward discussion, physical action being minimized and the dialogue centering on a "topic." In fact, a transitional stage between the two could be created by asking students to discuss a topic while assuming a certain social role or personality other than their own, perhaps that of a character in a book.

The size of discussion groups should be small, a group of no more than six taken aside by the teacher while the rest of the class is doing something else. Sometimes several such groups might be discussing at the same time, if they have had enough experience and if space permits. Occasionally, discussions by the whole class or half of it are worthwhile, especially when preparing to launch subgroups into separate work on a project or when bringing them back together to exchange results and combine experiences. In general, large groups are poor for *learning* to discuss and can only reap the benefits of this learning.

What the group discusses may be a book they have read in common, a student paper, an improvisation or performance by some of its members, an abstract topic of general interest, or many other things. I am concerned here with *how* they talk, with honing a fine cognitive tool out of extemporaneous conversation. The teacher's special talent, for which he must be trained, is to play a dialogue by ear and exploit the unforeseen twists and turns of it to explore all those things that textbooks ineffectually try to present to students in an exposition. Discussion of student and professional writing, for example, will naturally raise issues of what we call rhetoric, style, logic, semantics, grammar, literary form, and composition. What a student of language needs is not external facts but more insight about what he and his peers are doing verbally and what they could be doing. The teacher's knowledge of linguistics, semantics, or literary form, say, must influence the student. But the best method of influence is dramatic, not expository. The teacher's art is to open up the whole range of external, social operations that will lead to internal, cognitive operations. He does this by getting students to feed back to each other. Once they are independent of him, he may inject more of his experience into the conversation; but because such monologues should arise directly from their dialogue, the monologues can't be planned. The group should collaboratively forge serviceable abstractions and thus enable each member to do so alone.

The composition of groups — and hence of classes — should be as varied as possible. Individuals would be in one group formed for one purpose and in another formed for another purpose. But for the sake of a rich multiplicity of dialects, vocabulary, styles, ideas, and points of view, the class should be heterogeneously sectioned from a diverse student population. It should constitute the most powerful multilingual assembly that can be brought together. This means mixing levels of ability and achievement, mixing sexes, mixing races, and mixing socioeconomic classes. At times even ages should be temporarily mixed, and outside adults should come in and join discussions. Certainly the internalization process is severely curtailed if urban and suburban children, advantaged and disadvantaged, do not talk together. Not only will they have to "speak each other's language" in the future, for social and political reasons, but the language of each needs something from the other. Disadvantaged urban children can learn standard English only by speaking with people who use it. But, which is more important, they need to learn new *uses* of language — how to think by means of it, solve problems with it, influence others, and bring about action. Advantaged children living in *sub*urban ghettos will not be sacrificed by mixing. They need to relearn constantly the emotive and communal uses of language that middle-class upbringing tends to destroy. And their language needs the mythic and metaphoric qualities of lower-class speech. But all this means breaking the socioeconomic gerrymandering of large cities and restructuring school districts along metropolitan rather than municipal lines. If the educational ideal is to expand to the fullest the verbal and cognitive repertory of students, then the biggest single obstacle is ingrouping of all sorts, from familial to cultural.

Group discussion is a fundamental activity that should be a staple learning process from kindergarten through college. It is an activity to be learned both for its own sake and for the sake of learning other things by means of it. It is a major source of that discourse which the student will transform internally into thought. To do and be these things, it must become a highly wrought tool considerably different from what generally passes in schools today for "class discussion." To be clear about "right kind of dialogue," let me contrast current practices with some other models.

First of all, with rare exceptions most "class discussions" are actually serial dialogues between teacher and student A, then student B, etc. The model for this kind of exchange is the furniture arrangement — a block of little desks all facing the teacher's desk, which is isolated in front. The assumption seems to be that students can learn only from the teacher. There are several faults in the assumption and in that kind of conversation. For one thing, the proper development of thought requires operations other than question and answer — those corresponding, for example, to the additive, adversative, conditional, and concessive constructions of language. And usually the student is on one end only of the operation, the answer end. Think too of the multiplicity of attitudes represented by any mixed class of twenty or thirty students — the range of points of view and emendations going to waste. These do not have to be emitted by a teacher, and indeed often they could not be. Furthermore, emendation by the authority figure frequently elicits resistance because the student may associate it with "big people always trying to tell you what to do — even what to think."

The teacher should promote honest student-to-student conversation. His job is to help students learn from each other. If each student has to get clearance from the teacher to speak, interaction among students has little chance to take place. The raising of hands should be abolished but a ground rule of not interrupting held to. Small children will perhaps want to talk at once, and the beginning might be difficult, but if we are to convert "collective monologues" — simultaneous egocentric speeches — into real dialogue, the pupils must learn to listen and to respond to external as well as internal stimuli. Most of the furious flagging of hands and clamorous talking at once in traditional classes is actually provoked by the teacher, who usually has asked a question to which he knows the answer. The children, in competitively bidding for the teacher's approval, place no value on what other children say. The teacher must shed this parental role as dispenser of rewards and punishments and quit exploiting sibling rivalry to get right answers. It is ridiculously naive to construe as learning fervor the efforts of children to find psychic security.

Many teachers equate discussion with head-on contention. A "hot debate" is considered ideal even if it is a deadening clash of fixed ideas or a feverish struggle of egos. Cognitive development requires much more than sheer contention, which represents only the adversative operation and which frequently just solidifies everyone's ideas. Good discussion is chiefly qualifying statements, looking for what one *can* accept in an assertion and determining what one *cannot* accept. There is practically no statement one can think of that does not have some truth potential if properly qualified. The art is to stipulate the exact conditions under which some proposition *is* true, starting perhaps with the time, place, people, and circumstances to which it actually applies; then to quantify it (*all, some*); then to amend it with conditional, concessive, and proviso clauses. Vapid conclusions such as "it all depends on the individual" and "it's just a matter of semantics" are no substitute for trying to tailor a linguistic utterance to fit the reality one is talking about.

Good discussion also includes the "rules of evidence." Besides qualification, the only process that makes the difference between sound argumentation and a boring reiteration of opinions is invoking some material or logical reasons for accepting a statement. Evidence may be a narrative or anecdote, a syllogism, or a citation of some authoritative judgment or finding. The presence or absence of evidence, the nature of it, and the validity of it should become issues in the small groups.

Although formal debate as practiced by clubs and diplomats may help teach the presenting of evidence, I'm afraid I must take a strong stand against this kind of discourse in education. When someone is assigned in advance a position to champion, come hell or high water, the main point quickly becomes contention, not the search for truth. Formal debate is a game of one-upmanship, an unproductive duel of personalities. The goal is to overwhelm the opposition, not to enlarge one's mind. In my experience, debating societies always include in their membership the most dogmatic students in a school, who are drawn to such an activity because it offers an easy identity and an outlet for their talents of rationalization. It is true that part of debating is to learn to argue either side and to foresee the opponent's arguments, but this incorporation of the other's point of view is much better accomplished when one is not obliged by a prior investment to defend against that other point of view. I have several other objections to formal debating: both the dualistic format and the yes-or-no wording of topics cast issues in a crude either-or way that militates against relativistic thinking; the two parties often do not talk to the same point because their speeches are prepared; there is no feedback or interaction except in the rebuttal; and the speakers are in effect learning to ignore and talk past each other, an all too common trait of everyday conversation and diplomacy.

I am of course not trying to kill controversy. People do have and will maintain points of view in which, for one reason or another, they have an investment. What needs to be fostered, partly through controversy, is multiplicity of ideas, fertility, choice. The principle I am invoking is the old concept of the open market of ideas. A two-valued, prestructured, precommitted discourse does not live up to this principle. As an adversary game like chess or tennis, debate is fine, but it should not be a model for learning dialogue, which must include more than the adversative. Taking a position is not difficult and hardly needs to be taught; it comes to us readily with our natural egocentrism and ethnocentrism. What takes learning is the sense of alternative possibilities and the reasons for choosing one over another. Real truth-seeking has always been a collaboration of receptive minds; it requires a willingness *to be influenced*, reciprocity, which is a strength not a weakness. It is the lack of this honest ingredient that leads to so many international deadlocks: one wants to manipulate the other fellow and remain unchanged oneself. This sort of "debate" is mere propaganda. Certainly the social needs of the future will exact a superior kind of dialogue than we have taught and learned in the past. The threat that collaborative conversation poses to the ego is loss of identity, but it is patent that identity can and must be based on something more enduring than a certain ideological stance.

To characterize the kind of group operation I have in mind, I need to compare it to two rather well-known models. One is the kind of workshop long employed for apprentice actors, dancers, and craftsmen. The master sets the tasks (initially anyway), the apprentices present their productions to the group, and they all explore together the issues entailed by the tasks. The content is the students' productions and some brought in from the outside. The teacher's role is the natural one he has by virtue of being more experienced in the craft; he talks freely at times like any other member but does not feel obliged to pre-schedule what is to be talked about (his tasks may do this in a general way) or to center discussion around himself. He fosters cross-education among the students, and they focus on the tasks, not the teacher. Each learns both from garnering reactions to his own work and from reacting in turn to the work of others. All become highly involved in what the others are doing, not only because they are engaged in the same tasks but, more importantly, because they are a social unit that is allowed to be precisely that.

The other model is the "awareness group," one offshoot of the manifold thing called group dynamics. Whereas group therapy may release psychic forces that only a psychiatrist should be expected to manage, other kinds of dynamics have been successfully used in many practical groups, such as management training, to induce awareness in individuals of what roles they automatically take in a group, how others are reacting to them, how they are attempting to handle certain social relations, and what motives lie behind their own responses to others' behavior. Such things govern the kinds of co-operations that can take place. In other words, instead of ignoring the underlying drama of what is happening among the communicants and steamrolling ahead to get on with the "business," the "business" is construed as including both the objective task and the drama engendered in working on that task. The investments that corporations, institutions, and the armed services have made in such training attest to its practicality. Of course, it is up to classroom experimentation to establish the kind and degree of insight appropriate for different ages, but some steady source of insight is indispensable. Miscommunication, poor collaboration, and distortion of the task will occur if the human relations of the class are ignored or dealt with summarily as though they were a mere nuisance.

Furthermore, the awareness group is practical for language teaching in another way: a class is, like any constituted group, a miniature communication system; if the members pay attention to its workings, they can learn more about what makes and breaks communication than any book on the subject can possibly get across. The connection with the theater is closer than one might suspect. A playwright presents a model of our behavior — especially verbal behavior — so contrived as to reveal what is *really* happening, to give insights about motive, relationship, and interaction. What makes these insights so difficult to achieve in the heat of real life is our inability to act and see simultaneously. Witnessing a play, we have an opportunity to *see*. But if the ground rules of a group permit halting the action to review it a moment, and deflecting attention from content to people, then individuals can overcome participation-blindness and attain some of the insights afforded in the theater. A duality defines such a group, then — between involvement and detachment, between the communication and the metacommunication, the exposition and the drama.

The teacher's role in small group discussions shifts as students mature and acquire conversing experience.[6] In the beginning, it is to guide the *process* without contributing to the *substance* of the conversation; later when students can run the process themselves and can express themselves independently of the teacher's viewpoint, the teacher may either leave them to themselves or participate on an equal footing and say what he really thinks. Guiding the process consists of light organizing and prompting: the teacher helps the group settle on a topic they understand in the same way; calls attention to marked irrelevance, definitional misunderstanding, and personal relations thwarting the talk; occasionally draws in shyer members; and suggests other strategies when a given line of attack on a topic has proven fruitless. With older students, the teacher may continue to induce awareness of structural and interpersonal

---

[6] For some clarification of this role I have benefited from reading Babette Whipple, *The Grouptalk,* Occasional Paper #10 (Watertown, Mass.: Educational Development Corporation, January 1967). Though developed in a social studies program, her method is quite relevant to any course of verbal and cognitive learning.

difficulties while at the same time demonstrating by example the best ways of commenting and questioning substantively. Experience in dramatic improvisation, also, should help develop desirable characteristics of discussion such as attending closely, participating freely, responding directly, and interplaying rhetorically.

Thoroughly experienced and confident in unwitnessed discussion, the small group might converse before the rest of the class and thus become a panel, in the same way unwitnessed improvisations eventually become performances. Such a panel remains spontaneous and undivided into camps or teams. The witnessing portion of the class is provided with a detached relationship to the communicants and their ideas; this should make for calmer assessment of the ideas presented and greater awareness of dynamics in the large group. When the panel is over, the spectators can discuss both the dialectic and the drama of the panelists. Also, representatives from each small group may constitute a panel charged with discussing further what each group has discussed. This cross-fertilizes ideas from different groups.

Performing Scripts

Performing planned plays, written by either professionals or students, is a natural concomitant of improvising. Improvisation should make acting performances better, but performance creates new problems, such as memorizing the script and blocking the action, that are peculiar to planned drama. Although rehearsals take more time, they are more worthwhile than sight readings, which are rendered rather ineffectual by stumbling reading and encumbrance with the script. Short one-acters written by students would often serve well, and subsequent discussion of the performance could relate acting to writing. Putting on professional plays makes for more effective and pleasurable literary study than reading them, at least until students have had enough experience participating and witnessing to be able to bring the script to life in their minds. Performing a play offers the same opportunities as improvisation to play different roles, to attitudinize, and to develop fluency, but it may be an easier way for some students because the words and deeds are already given. Last, in memorizing and speaking lines for a script, a student is internalizing the language, style, thought, and point of view of a voice and personality probably different from his own.

I will not speak at length about play performing because it is commonly done in schools. But I will call attention to mistaken views of it or neglected aspects.

First, the point of performing is the learning experience it provides, not showing off to parents and the public. Too often performance is limited to a rare big production for presentation to outsiders and is relegated to extracurricular activities. I think there should be much more in-class performing of small pieces — short student scripts and scenes from professional plays. Small groups could exchange scripts, or choose scenes, discuss them, and work up a production, each group performing in turn.

Second, play performance should be interwoven with improvisation and script writing, not just come as climax or dessert to the reading of a play. Improvisations on a similar situation may be necessary to insure comprehension of a scene or involvement with it. And acting and writing can illuminate each other.

Third, besides student and professional play scripts, short stories, and many poems are also candidates for performance. With short stories, the *narrator* as well as the characters is assigned an actor. Thus, in addition to speaking the dialogue and enacting the movement, the performers also give stage voice to the speaker of the story. This method, which has been beautifully worked out in a technique called Chamber Theater,[7] permits the dramatizing of different narrator-character relationships and hence of fictional point of view. As for poems, many

---

[7] Carolyn Fitchett, "An English Unit. Chamber Theater Technique," Unpublished but copyrighted 1966 by the Program for Pre-College Centers, a division of Educational Development Corporation. The technique was introduced by Professor Robert S. Breen of Northwestern University and further developed by Miss Fitchett.

are soliloquy, dramatic monologue, or dialogue and can be performed as they are; many more are narratives that can be performed in the Chamber Theater technique used for fiction.

Monologuing

The last of the vocal activities is monologuing. While becoming fluent in the give and take of conversation, a student should be induced to detach himself from the group and to talk alone. Giving a prepared speech is an act of composition followed by a reading; delivery is not what I have in mind here, but rather a kind of spontaneous monologue that would prepare for composition. As a gradual weaning, I suggest letting individuals take over the conversation for longer and longer duration, to supply anecdotes or special knowledge they may have about some aspect of a subject that is before the group. If the discussion is on transportation, the child of a bus driver might be asked to relay things his father has told him. Reading aloud one's written composition is also an easy habituation to monologuing. Next, individuals would be asked to summarize a panel or group discussion, a more difficult organizing task than telling a narrative. With more meaningful ground rules, the show-and-tell sessions could also serve to develop powers of monologue. That is, a student who has brought something to class is somewhat in the expert's position and therefore a logical monologuist, but without involved questions from his peers he may just mutter a few words and the matter will end with "How nice." There is no reason for show-and-tell not to continue into the later years. As strong hobbies and competencies grow, older children will have a lot more to say about the things they bring in — how they work, the history, procedures, etc. — things that provide a natural outline of an extended utterance but that don't need to be prepared. It is better to let the student present his information spontanously and for him to learn, through questions and other feedback, what might have been a better way to say what he had to say. Such a monologue could serve as the base for a written piece later.

Recording

I think it is clear how drama, narrative, exposition, and argumentation can be learned in some measure without writing a word, through oral improvisation. The oral activities are basic but not in the sense of being limited to elementary school alone; I think they should be interwoven with writing throughout secondary school as well. The activities I am going to take up now would constitute some of the early writing but would also recur as later assignments too. In rough summary these activities are two — eyewitness recording and playwriting. Of course, considered as productions by one individual, both are monological; that is, the student must enchain the utterances by himself. But both recording and invented dialogue are based on the same enchainment — time order of occurrence, the simplest of all. "Then . . . then." Then I see this. Then he says this. The difference is that an eyewitness has fewer decisions to make about what to put down than a playwright, because the events are given and not invented.

For recording, the student is placed in an observer relation to some phenomena and asked to dictate or write down what he registers with his senses at a particular time and place. The result is a kind of perceptual soliloquy, either in the form of telegraphic notations or of more leisurely sentences. The key tense is the progressive present; the student is verbalizing *as* he registers, and that is the definition of recording. The records thus produced are aimed at no other audience than himself and are not to be judged as communications, which they do not purport to be.

The three-fold purpose is to develop powers of observation, produce material that can subsequently be rewritten for an outside audience, and learn to abstract sensations into words. Perceptual abstraction is the first stage of symbolizing conscious experience and a necessary condition for thinking and writing. Many so-called *writing* faults, such as lack of detail, lack of example, indiscrimination, and inaccuracy are traceable to poor observation. Starting with raw sensory data well nigh eliminates stale imitation and thus increases originality. Also, in order to become aware of how he processes information all the time, the student needs to examine *all* phases of his abstracting. Selected and told from a later point of view, a record becomes a narrative of either a personal or scientific sort. Or the notations can become the stage directions and action of a play. A sound record among people may produce an actual dialogue. In other words, a recording may be used almost as is, or it may be abstracted to further levels for different purposes and audiences. The student learns that material for writing is all around him at any given moment. The problem of prewriting — finding subjects and treating them in stages that lead to a finished product — can be solved, I believe, by spontaneous recording, which is another kind of improvisation.

The stimuli for recordings can be provided to some extent within the classroom, for children young enough to need such structuring, but ultimately it is desirable for students to choose a time and place outside of class to do their recording. Animals, mechanical contraptions, science demonstrations, pantomimists — anything that moves — can serve in the structured situation. The shift from teacher-selected to student-selected stimuli can accompany a shift from isolated senses to interplay of senses. That is, first a student is asked to record only what he hears, or sees, or touches, of what is presented in school, and then to record all his sensations somewhere away from school.

Students unable to write can dictate their verbalized sensations to the teacher or to older students. In fact, it might be better for any student who is concentrating on sounds or touch to close his eyes and dictate to a partner who would then trade places with him. The dictation itself can be a strong learning device, since it entails breaking the flow of speech sounds into words and other units; spelling, punctuation, and accuracy of quotation can then be gone over together by the partners. (This practice can be related in turn to recording dialogue.) Expedients have to be devised for somehow capturing events that happen too fast to keep up with otherwise. The problem is the same for someone recording sights and sounds as it is for someone playing stenographer; both are in a sense taking dictation. By reading and discussing their records, students can explore telegraphic and fuller styles, the best ways to capture sensations hurriedly, options of word choice, and the degree of dispensability of different parts of speech. They can also discuss the advantages of composing after the fact and the various ways of rewriting that would be required to make a record understandable and interesting to another audience.

In fact, a teacher can exploit recording for virtually anything he wishes to teach — linguistics, semantics, point of view, description, narrative. By varying the speed and conditions of the assignment, he can bring different linguistic structures under scrutiny. By asking several students to record at the same time and place, he can work with the different ways students name the same phenomena, differences in their perceptual selections and differences in their physical vantage points. If, just after a pantomime performance, the spectators write down what they think it was they witnessed, they can discuss their different interpretations and relate these differences to ambiguities in the acting and to idiosyncrasies of recording. Recordings made by the same student at the same place but at a different time can be compared also. If students are asked to spot personal judgments in their own and others' recordings, they become adept at separating physical fact from inferences and interposed attitudes — or at least at discovering the subtle interrelations of these things. They should be led to contemplate the way what we see is influenced by our wants, prior interests, and conventions — how concept influences percept.

Since the order of utterances is determined by the order of events, recordings are chronological, but in two ways. An active scene bombards the observer with an external order of events, whereas a still life tableau forces the observer to fall back on the order of his own body movements. That is, contrary to what composition texts say about static description, there is no such thing as *spatial* order. Only time can order in the physical world. The order of items in a still life description is determined by the observer's attentional sequence — either his movement in that space, the movement of his head and eyeballs, or the idiosyncrasies of his perceptual selections, which may be partly conceptual. In short, we have a record either of external events beyond the observer's control or of the observer's actions themselves.

Students ready to look inward somewhat can be asked to record, first, their internal sensations, then their flow of memories, then their flow of thoughts. Many young people, and adults, are unaware of what they are feeling, kinesthetically and emotionally, until they consciously turn attention inward to the organs and other parts of the body. Then they notice little aches, itches, and muscular tensions, or emotions as manifested by physical sensations. Next, using immediate surroundings as stimuli to trigger past sensations, the student begins writing down trains of memories and, eventually, trains of thought associations. Although memories concern what happened and reflections concern what happens or may happen, the *act* of remembering or reflecting is a part of what is happening now, and like any other events of the present can be recorded as it goes on. The gradual shift of focus inward is one curriculum progression; another is the sensations-memory-reflections sequence, which mounts the abstraction ladder of symbolic activities.

The inner verbal system called soliloquy is really a mixture of currents, but by focusing attention on one of these currents we can make it nearly exclude the others, temporarily. This happens naturally all the time — as inner and outer events "call attention to themselves"; what the teacher's assignment does is act as an outside influence that helps the student tap these currents for their rich and individualistic materials. Furthermore, a lot of the stream is actually subverbal or perhaps unconscious and does not really become soliloquy until an effort of attention brings it to the word level.

Writing Scripts and Dialogues

Taking dictation, recording behavior, and improvising dramas and discussions should all ease the way to play writing in two ways. One is in training the eye to note behavior and the ear to note speech; the other is in getting a sense of responsiveness and interplay among people. Trying to write plays should further develop such faculties as well as make the reading of plays a much more meaningful experience. What I will outline here is a suggested sequence of assignments in dramatic writing.

A good beginning is to invent a short, unbroken conversation between two people, what I call a duologue. The point is to get something interesting going between the people without worrying too much about wrapping up the ending in a big climax. (One kind of two-person drama is a monologue spoken to someone who does not speak.) From this point of departure the student progresses to a triadic relationship, which is already a lot more difficult to handle, and then on to a longer scene that mixes duets, trios, and quartets. He is encouraged to try soliloquies. He is told to limit stage directions to what the audience can see and hear. This is to prevent the amateur tendency to tell how characters feel and to insert abstract information. A severer limitation is to write the script with no stage directions, so that time, place, and circumstances must all come through the dialogue. In any case, until the student can write a dialogue for several voices that is indeed dramatic, it seems a good idea to hold the play to one continuous scene. This can produce one-acters, and even if the student stops here he has learned a lot. The next step is to write a play of several scenes. This complexity brings on problems of plotting and selection that approach similar problems in narrative. Which action is to occur offstage and which on? How is the offstage action to be summarized for the audience? Pacing also becomes more difficult along with the effective juxtaposing of scenes of different times and places. Whatever the degree of complexity, it is important that the writer draw his characters, action, and setting from a world he has some knowledge of; otherwise he draws on all the movies and TV shows he has seen.

Writing Socratic dialogues can build a bridge from drama to essays of ideas. The student designates two voices as A and B and writes a dialogue between them about some topic he or the class has chosen. The topic might be something about what the class has been reading. This conversation is improvised straight off on paper for about a half hour. The purpose is to turn over a subject and get different points of view on it. Older students could work with three or four voices. Doing this alone on paper presupposes a lot of oral experience. It asks, in effect, that the student bring out and put into play whatever points of view he has stored, without fear of contradicting himself. After writing ideas in this dialogue manner, he can proceed to self-consistent monological essays.

Another sequence, parallel, goes from collaborative to individual script writing. Before reaching the stage of simply sitting down and writing a play alone, a student should first be allowed to help a script evolve out of small-group improvisation. After improvising several versions of a situation, the group discusses and drafts together a script of their favorite version. This might be given to another group to perform.

Before passing on to the receptive activities, I think I should make it clear that the purpose of asking students to write in play form, or in any other literary form, is not to engender hordes of little creative writers. My concern is greater for a curriculum that helps semiliterate, nonverbal types of children than one that fosters the gifted. The very profound relationship that exists between literary and everyday discourse — some of which I hope I have demonstrated in this essay — is such that to work in one is to work in the other. Nearly all the assignments I am recommending have multiple goals. A student who writes a play is learning how to converse, to appreciate an art form, to understand himself, to describe, and, very generally, simply to write. Let's look at these goals a moment.

To begin with the last, creating a play script allows a young student to write a lot of colloquial speech at a time when he may not be ready to compose more formal sentences. He can write as people talk. Continuity and organization are relatively easy because the sequence of utterances need not be abstractly logical but can follow the familiar social give-and-take of conversation. And yet the writer is faced with the primary writing task of making sights out of sounds, of reproducing voice through orthography and punctuation. Writing dialogue is the best way to learn to punctuate. If it is clear that the script must enable someone else to read the lines as the author heard them in his head when he wrote them, then the author knows he must use typography as a set of signals indicating to a reader where the stresses and pauses are and how the intonation goes. This is what the breaking and punctuating of sentences on the page is all about anyway. The rules are merely an attempt to generalize the relations between sound, syntax, and sense. But no one ever has trouble punctuating orally; the problem is rendering speech on the page. Children who don't learn how to punctuate in twelve years of rules could learn in a few months by having other students *mis*read their own dialogues back to them. The problem is one of egocentrism: hearing in his own head the correct intonation and pauses of an utterance he is writing, the author doesn't realize that someone else is likely to impose a different reading unless he is guided by typographical cues. Overcoming such egocentrism requires, first, an awareness of what he is hearing himself, and then an awareness that the other person does not know what he knows. Both spelling and punctuation can be worked on by subgroups of students reading and diagnosing each other's dialogues — once the teacher has focused them, with some examples, on the real issues involved. A language teacher is not a proofreader and should never become one.

Stage directions are a combination of narrative and description. The referents are physical. Although the narrative part can follow chronological order and is central to the action, the description is intermittent and accessory, as is the case for description generally. Above all, therefore, it must be relevant and significant, well selected and well timed. A natural criterion is that the physical appearance of a character or a setting should relate to the action and to the author's purpose. What should be the order of items, and therefore of utterances, when telling how something looks when it does not move? This is a good task and one that goes beyond the logic of time.

All I will say about learning to converse through playwriting is that writing dialogue activates one's repertory of potential voices and gives practice in building conversations with these voices.

Understanding art and understanding oneself I want to take together and apply beyond drama, for the sake of a general educational principle, which is to let students write their own literature. Although one very reasonable argument for this principle is that students can often write better and more appropriate reading material for each other than is manufactured for them by some adult writers of primers, my case rests on a couple of more important beliefs. They are that a student who role-plays the artist (1) comes to appreciate and understand the art form intuitively without needing teacher explanation and tedious vivisections and postmortems, and (2) that some of the benefits that accrue to the artist accrue to him. Anyone who has written some duologues and triologues, or one-acters, or a whole play is much more likely to grasp for himself what the dynamics is of a certain moment in Ibsen or Shakespeare, what the main vector is of a certain scene, or its purpose, why some scenes occur offstage and some on, how people's speech characterizes them, what the importance is of setting and objects, what a clumsy or expert exposition is, and so on. The same is true with fiction and poetry. Most inexperienced students take all the decisions of the artist for granted. In fact, they see no choice, only arbitrariness or inevitability. Appreciation of form comes only with a sense of the choices — from the selection of persona, locale, and events to who goes offstage when and what gesture accompanies which speech. When you yourself invent, you see all the choices, make decisions; the arbitrariness and inevitability of what professionals do disappears. It all begins to make sense. You are on the inside of the game, and it is more fun to play this way. When you discuss a professional play in class, you are motivated to talk about how the author says what happens by presenting what is happening. Because you know what he is doing, you know what he is saying.

The benefits an artist enjoys concern the exploitation and controlling of his fantasies for an objective connection and for self-knowledge. Fantasies are one kind of abstracting, and the purpose of abstracting is to reduce reality to something manageable. Children, like adults, make their way in the world and among their own feelings by creating some abstractions that help manage reality. They will fantasy anyway; all the teacher is asking them to do is shape some of these fantasies in words and forms which are public. An artist externalizes his fantasies, sells them for profit, and at the same time gets a chance to examine them and have them examined. All people seem to feel a vital need to find correspondences, "objective correlatives," between mind and world. Perhaps this is partly in order to get in touch with less conscious parts of themselves, but it is partly, I think, just to connect for its own sake. To plug inner experience into outside equivalents seems to be of profound importance for human beings. Otherwise it is difficult to account for the addiction both children and adults have for stories, in whatever medium. Instead of merely projecting *into* someone else's inventions, the artist projects his own. The advantage is greater personal accuracy and appropriateness of fantasy to feeling. One of the benefits to the student as artist, then, is creating symbols through which to correspond with the outside world, and by which he can learn about himself. Once externalized in public, i.e. impersonal, forms, ideas and feelings can be dealt with, changed, and resolved. For less verbal children such expression may be more important than for the talented.

Creating fictions, imaginatively recombining real elements, is thinking. The fact that these elements may be characters, events, and objects does not make a literary construction less an act of thought than any other kind of abstraction. Art is simply a different *mode* of abstracting. It is a great mistake for the teacher to imagine an opposition between "creative" writing and idea writing. The ideas in plays and novels may not be named, as in exposition, but they are there. They are implicit in the selection, arrangement, and patterning of events and character.

The art is to *embody* ideas. And the child's first grasping of ideas is through embodiments of them. A student writing a play automatically makes it a way of saying something; there has to be something determining his choices. Whereas recording grounds discourse in reality, inventing allows a student to recombine things in ways he has not witnessed and thus opens the realm of possibility. This is the precursor for advanced logic, which consists of permuting knowns as to arrive at unknowns.

Reading

Of the three input activities two have already been dealt with above — listening and witnessing. When some students are improvising a drama or panel, or performing a play, the others are looking on. Recording, taking dictation, and interacting in conversation all develop alertness and receptivity. I need add only the important experience of listening to tapes and discs and watching films. Professional recordings and films of plays are of course an excellent way to bring alive dramatic literature, but I would recommend in particular the practice of playing a recording of a play, poem, or story while the students follow the text. This gives real voice to the words on the page and thus enables the student to *hear* meaning and emotion as well as pronunciation and the intonation patterns of both colloquial and literary discourse. Such tight binding of sound, sight, and sense should improve silent reading and comprehension of the text, strengthen the internalization of new language forms and vocabulary, and increase involvement with literature. In lieu of professional recordings, local tape recordings can be made by teachers, other adults, or talented students.

There is another kind of drama that has seldom been tapped for classroom use. It is the ceaseless production of court rooms, hearings, senate committee investigations, and actual panel discussions. These are not only dramatic in the general sense but also often downright theatrical. They illustrate beautifully the tight relation between interplay of roles and personalities and the dialectic of ideas. At the same time as they deal seriously with important ideas, they forcefully enact the dynamics of groups. I think that curriculum builders should make a great effort to obtain transcripts, tapes, and videotapes of these real-life dialogues. These could be heard, seen, and read in conjunction with the performing and reading of dramatic literature. Students should understand clearly both the similarities and differences between everyday, spontaneous dialogues and composed, literary plays. Though the theater simulates real behavior, at some degree of remove, it also harmonizes, resolves, relates, and transforms it. While seeing the unreality of realism, the artifice of art, the student can at the same time appreciate the organic relevance of plays to life.

Reading a play alone should occur only after improvising and performing plays and should be interwoven with the writing of dramatic pieces and the witnessing of professional performances. Until a student has had the experience of hearing and seeing plays and being in them, an experience that enables him to bring the script alive in his imagination, the reading of plays is not very rewarding and creates unnecessary problems of incomprehension. The failure of most play teaching is due to this lack of preparation. The text of a play leaves the reader more on his own than most narratives, which describe, guide, and explain more. A script requires a lot of inference. On the page, a young reader doesn't "see" where X is standing when he is delivering a certain line, or who he is saying it to, or which actions are taking place concurrently. Nor does he "hear" the significant inflections or tones of voice. If this is so for modern plays, it is true *a fortiori* for Shakespearean texts, which have few stage directions. Generally, no narrator provides continuity between scenes or says what people are thinking or hints at their motives. A rough sequence, then, is from the boards to the book, but always returning to the boards (or film or tape) as often as possible.

Once the reading is launched, however, a more specific sequence is possible, the one outlined for the writing of plays. It goes from simple to complex but not by dint of extracting parts from plays. In fact, the idea is never to assign anything less than a complete play but to choose, in the beginning, whole short plays that in effect constitute the building blocks of larger, more complex plays, that is, to find works of dramatic literature that are monologue, duologue, or triologue unfolding continuously at one time and place. These are one-scene plays limited to very few voices and hence to a simpler psychological dynamics. From this point progression is toward increasing number of voices and relations, more complex orchestration of *groups* of voices, and increasing extension of the action in time and space. The farther flung a play — the more scenes it has occurring at different times and places, and the larger the cast — the more the play becomes narrative and expository. That is, plot becomes more important, interim action must be summarized, the relations of scenes made clear, the identities of new characters conveyed, and their relevance explained. Whereas the more here and now, the more dramatic.

If we include within drama a lot of poetry that purports to be a recording of persona voices speaking now — interior monologues, dramatic monologues, and duologues — we enlarge the repertory of whole short works. The test is whether they could be put on stage. Soliloquies like "Soliloquy of a Spanish Cloister," "Ode to a Nightingale," "The Love Song of J. Alfred Prufrock," and "Ulysses"; dramatic monologues like "My Last Duchess," "The Ballad of the Goodly Fere," and "To His Coy Mistress"; mixed interior and dramatic monologues like Henry Reed's "Naming of Parts"; duologues like "Lord Randall," "Ulysses and the Sirens," "Ann Gregory," Reed's "Judging Distances," and "West-Running Brook" all could be performed. So long as the poem presents the unintroduced, uninterrupted transcription of what some characters are saying at a certain time or place or in certain circumstances, it is dramatic. Many poems are difficult for students to understand simply because they do not expect drama in a poem and immediately assume that the voice they hear is the author's and that he is philosophizing. "My Last Duchess," which even my bright eleventh graders seldom understood on the page, would be very comprehensible if two people acted it out — one gesturing to a portrait and speaking about it while the other reacted with growing revulsion until he finally started prematurely down the stairs. In fact, some short stories are interior and dramatic monologues and differ from some of these poems only in being in prose. My point could best be made if the reader were to compare the text of "My Last Duchess" with that of Strindberg's play *The Stronger* and George Milburn's story "The Apostate," each of which has one speaker and one silent reactor. When a work is clearly dramatic, it should be taught as such, regardless of the genre under which it is classified. And a lot of literature that could *not* be performed is better understood on the page if the student is used to characterizing and situating voices and to shifting from one voice to another.

Rhetoric

Several teaching issues relate to all of the activities and methods which I have been dealing with up to this point. They concern general aspects of discourse. One of these is rhetoric.

For me *rhetoric* refers to the ways one person attempts to act on another, to make him laugh or think, squirm or thrill, hate or mate. Unlike other animals, the human baby cannot for some time do for itself. During the first months of utter helplessness and the following years of extreme dependence, the child must get others to do for it. Thus we learn at the outset of life the tremendously important art of manipulating other people. This is the genesis of rhetoric — and it begins before we learn to speak. Crying soon becomes a means of summoning the milk supply or the dry diaper. Later the rhetorical repertory of the child includes vomiting, holding breath, throwing temper tantrums, evacuating inappropriately, whining, wheedling — and obeying. Acting on others through words is merely one aspect of the larger rhetoric of behavior.

Now, although we are concerned here with acting on others through words only, the fact is that, as a specialization of general instrumental behavior, verbal rhetoric originates in mixture with other behavior — as on the stage — and only later, when we learn to monologue in writing, does it isolate itself.

The guts of drama is rhetoric, people acting on each other; speech is featured but nonverbal influence is highly prized, to say the least. A play is a model of how the student, his parents, friends, and enemies do things to each other verbally and in conjunction with gesture, voice, and movement. In a play the communicants are "live," existential; the personalities behind the words are the most real, the intentions and ploys the most evident. Everything is *present*. Drama is the perfect place to begin the study of rhetoric. Confronted with a written monologue — a novel, essay, or treatise — a student deals with a phantom by comparison. An essay has a speaker who in turn has motives and ways of acting on his audience. But this action-at-a-distance will be much harder to recognize and respond to if the student has not been long accustomed, through experience with drama, to link words to speakers to motives. Reading, witnessing, and discussing plays will sensitize him to rhetoric, and he should also practice it himself, in his own voice and in invented voices, by improvising, writing, and performing dramas. Even if our student is destined to write nothing more than notes to the milkman, or to discourse only orally, he can at least learn to do these things effectively through a developed rhetoric and become aware that what is bombarding him through the mass media issues from people who have designs on him. Although we enter school already with a rhetoric, it is of course naive and drastically inadequate to later communication needs. The function of the school is to extend the rhetorical repertory and to bind messages so tightly to message senders that this relation will not be lost in transferring it to the page. What is too obvious to notice in conversation must be raised to a level of operational awareness that will permit this transfer.

Style

Closely related to how A acts on B through words is A's choice of diction, phrasing, sentence structure, and organization — his style. The best preparation for discriminating styles on the page is to become attuned to them in person. Reading is listening to somebody talk. This does not mean that we write in just the same way as we talk, but simply that writing is monologuing. In fact, the special qualities of writing are best understood when seen as changes in diction, phrasing, sentence structure, and organization made, precisely, in order to adjust to the loss of vocal and facial expression, gesticulation, feedback, collaboration, and the other characteristics of conversation. Ideally, as one reads he would hear a voice and conjure a person who would be uttering it. This person would be someone capable of saying such things in such ways. To teach style I would emphasize the continuity between dramatis personae in plays and the admittedly paler personae who are the authors of written monologues.

One is unlikely, however, to detect stylistic differences if one hears no more than one style, just as one is not likely to detect phonetic distinctions made in other languages but not in one's own. This is another reason why students should be exposed in the classroom to a wide range of voices, dialects, and life styles, and why they should role-play different people. A style proceeds partly from a class and ethnic background, and partly from personal idiosyncrasy. Some of style is conditioned and some is a matter of changing wishes, as when a writer decides to take a debonair, foreboding, or satiric posture with a certain essay but not with another. Differences precede choice and choice precedes style. A student asked to take such and such a role in an improvisation realizes that he should try to "sound like" that persona. Writing dialogue requires differentiating the voices of various personae and applying the realistic criterion that words should match their speakers and the stances of the speakers. The educational principle involved here is that a thoroughgoing attunement to the styles of voices in the here-and-now makes it possible later to "hear" a style on the page. Also, out of a diverse dramatic experience the student can begin to develop choice, break through stereotyped conditioning, and create a voice that truly utters him.

The Drama of the Classroom

As for teaching language generally, a dramatic pedagogy is superior to an expository one. It seems terribly misguided to me to *tell about* something to students when they are *using* that something every day of their lives. As a school subject, language is unique in this way. In fact, it is truly language only when it *is* being used. It is not really a something at all; it is an action going on in somebody's head or between people. Words in a book are mere paper and ink until someone starts to read them. And he reads them only by virtue of a prior social activity. The expository approach would prepare textbooks and workbooks that either tell a student what he is already doing or tell him what he ought to be doing in his verbal behavior. Since this verbal behavior can be practiced in the same room in which it can be told or read about, the most sensible course, it seems to me, is to behave verbally and behave some more verbally about that behavior and thus modify and enlarge discourse in the ways the expository approach means to do (and in some ways doesn't mean to do). The prepared statements and exercises of textbooks never come at the right time to modify behavior; only something more extemporaneous can do that. To read and be told about, at one time and place, how language works and how we should best use it, then to try to discourse for real at another time and place . . . well, to make such an application and transfer presupposes an intellectual attainment that could only be the end not the means of an education. Correction and enlightenment "take" best when they come right in midtask, when the knowledge is just what one needs to know at that moment.

Besides being inefficient and irrelevant, exposition is inhumane. It is dull. In other subjects it may to some extent be unavoidable if the subject is a corpus of facts which the student cannot know any other way. But the facts and possibilities of discourse can be known in another way, one more akin to how the student has already been learning language and to how he will be using it out of school, except that this dramatic method can be used with a consciousness and deliberateness denied to the home and the marketplace.

As much as teachers may often wish that they could ignore, eliminate, or stylize into innocuousness the sociality of the classroom, they neither should do so nor can they. Ultimately a student, or adult for that matter, is more interested in his relation to other people than he is in a subject, because psychic survival and fulfillment depend on what kind of relation one works out with the social world. Since some life drives are at stake, no student is going to forsake this interest no matter how tough the discipline; the teacher can't control the student's mind. He will get interested in the subject to the extent that he can make it relevant to his current needs. Instead of creating constant tension between the social motives of the student and his own motive to teach the "subject," the teacher would do better to acknowledge that his own intellectual pursuits are framed by dramatic relations between him and the world, and to recognize that this must be true for his students as well. Since discourse is ultimately social in origin and in function, it seems a shame to fight those forces that could be put to such excellent use in teaching the subject.

CHAPTER FOUR |

Narrative: What Happened

Again, in this chapter, I would like to magnify a range of discourse, draw parallels between literature and everyday life, and work out in more detail some aspects of the general theory outlined earlier. Narrative occupies a considerable portion of the discursive spectrum, overlapping with drama, but not all of narrative is covered here — only those sorts having counterparts in fiction. I will stop short of broadly historical and typological narrative, which begin to bridge into explicit generalization. Indeed, the finer delineation of the upper ranges of the total discursive spectrum remains a task for the future.

The bulk of this chapter is reprinted from "Telling Stories: Methods of Abstraction in Fiction." Reprinted by permission from *ETC: A Review of General Semantics*, Vol. XXI, No. 4; copyright 1964 by the International Society for General Semantics. Other portions, written in collaboration with Kenneth R. McElheny, are reprinted by arrangement with The New American Library, Inc., from POINTS OF VIEW: AN ANTHOLOGY OF SHORT STORIES, edited by James Moffett and Kenneth McElheny. Copyright © 1966 by James Moffett and Kenneth R. McElheny. The stories in that anthology are grouped according to the classification of fictional techniques set forth in this chapter.

"What happened?" When we attempt to answer this question we become momentarily a story-teller. A friend asks, "What did you do yesterday?" A colleague asks what went on at a professional convention you attended. Or, more formally, we may report certain events in a newspaper or magazine, present a case history in a specialized journal, or write for the general reader a biography, memoir, or history.

The essence of story is once-upon-a-time. Once. Unique and unrepeatable events — not "recurring" events, as in science. Whether the events be made up or really happened makes no difference for what I am going to say, which concerns *how* we tell stories. All who set out to recount what happened — the historian and the fictionalist, the journalist and the case-writer, the man of law and the man in the street — share something in common: they all have some relation to the events and some relation to their audience. More basically than anything else, these two relations determine how we tell our stories.

Fiction writers, being people who like to talk anyway, do not wait to be asked, "What happened?" They just start in and tell you. But this is not their only aberration. The fiction artist differs from his soberer brethren in being more expert, not at communication, but at metacommunication, which is a word that he has probably never heard of (for in typical fashion he has left it to the scientist to name what he would just as soon not talk about, whereas the scientist may talk about such things, but of course he wouldn't touch the stuff himself).

Metacommunication is a set of more or less hidden signals that tell us where and when and how to look; the communication is what we are directed to look *at*. Form and content, if you prefer (or syntax and message, structure and substance, energy and mass, Yin and Yang). The novelist or short story writer turns the head of the reader with such cunning necromancy that, by comparison, the journalist and the lawyer look downright ingenuous with their slants and their biases. And of course historians and behavioral scientists don't use form, they just present objective content.

The artist knows innately, as the gamin knows how to steal, that *what* is merely a factor of *how*; that we can no more separate the story from the telling than, as Yeats said, we can tell the dancer from the dance. Events are human creations. Even when he claims to let the material speak for itself, the artist knows that he is just fooling the customers, that the great ongoing panorama of life does not speak at all — not until some human tongue begins to wag. So it is to that old snake-charmer, the fictioneer, that I turn for our lesson. By calling himself an artist and thus admitting that he is a low-down subjective cheat and a metacommunicative con man, he instructs us honest men how to stay honest. On the principle of a thief to catch a thief, let us look at a spectrum of fictional methods arrayed so as to "reveal" the different, but relative, forms of story-telling.

Each technique is illustrated by an excerpt from a short story or novel, the passage being typical of the technique employed throughout the entire work from which it is quoted. Before each passage I describe the technique abstractly. It is important to keep in mind that the illustrations merely sample the range of the spectrum, which may be infinitely graduated; the techniques blend one into another, according to gradual shifts in the rhetorical relation between speaker and audience, and the referential relation between speaker and subject. This sequence goes from the most subjective and personal to the most objective and impersonal, as regards both the speaker's relation to his listener and the speaker's relation to his subject. Thus it is based on varying relations among first, second, and third persons.

Significantly, there is also a progression up the abstraction ladder: (1) speaker, listener, and subject become gradually more diffused in time and space — more generalized; (2) each technique subsumes the previous ones and is built up out of them; in the same way classes include subclasses by increasing summary of primary moments of experience.

Narrative method is here defined as both a certain level of abstraction and as the communication system operating among teller, told-to, and told-about. The communication system expands throughout the sequence.

Other progressions are:

- From I to he, from informer to information.
- From present to past.
- From the I-you relation (drama) to the I-he relation (narrative)
- From double story to single story.
- From vernacular improvisation to literary composition.
- From intrapersonal communication to interpersonal communication to personal communication (identified speaker, anonymous audience) to impersonal communication (anonymous speaker, anonymous audience).
- Increasing time interval between date of events and date of narration, until time interval loses importance.
- Increasing distance (in all senses) between speaker and listener, then between speaker and subject.

Sequence of Narrative Types

I. Interior Monologue

An unintroduced, uninterrupted transcription of what some character situated in a given time and circumstance is perceiving and thinking. This amounts to intra-organismic communication, since the speaker is also listener; the reader is simply permitted to "tune in" on the communication. Strictly speaking, since this voice subdivides, a better name would be interior dialogue. The "story" is the *process* of perceiving and thinking at least as much as it is the content of the perceptions and thoughts.

WE'LL TO THE WOODS NO MORE[1]

By Edouard Dujardin

The menu. Let's see; fish, sole . . . yes, a sole. *Entrées,* mutton cutlets . . . no. Chicken . . . yes.

[1] Edouard Dujardin, WE'LL TO THE WOODS NO MORE, pp. 21–24. Translated by Stuart Gilbert. Copyright 1938 by New Directions. Reprinted by permission of New Directions Publishing Corporation. Dujardin is generally credited with inventing the interior monologue as a fictional technique, and, according to Dujardin, James Joyce acknowledged that his own use of the technique in *Ulysses* was inspired by *We'll to the Woods No More.*

— Sole. Then some chicken, with watercress.

— Yes, sir. Sole, chicken, and cress.

So I'm going to dine, and a very good idea too. Now that's a pretty woman over there; neither fair nor dark; a high-stepper, by gad; tallish, probably; must be the wife of that bald man with his back to me; more likely his mistress; somehow she hasn't just the married air; quite a pretty girl, really. She might look this way; almost exactly opposite me she is; what shall I? Oh, what's the good? There, she's spotted me. Really a pretty woman, and the man looks a bore; a pity I can only see his back; I'd like to have a look at his face too; lawyer, I should say, a family solicitor up from the country. Absurd I am! How about the soup? The glass in front of me reflects the gilded frame; the gilded frame behind me of course; those arabesques in bright vermillion, all scarlet flashes; but the light is pale yellow; walls, napery, mirrors, wine-glasses, all yellowed by the gaslight. It's comfortable here, well-appointed place. Here's the soup, piping hot; waiter might splash some, better keep an eye on him. All's well; let's begin. Too hot, this soup; wait, try again. Not half bad. I lunched a bit too late, no appetite left. All the same I must eat some dinner. Soup finished. That woman looked this way again; expressive eyes she has and the man with her seems a dull bird; I might get to know her by some fluke; queerer things happen; why not? If I keep on looking at her, it might lead to something; but they've reached the joint already; never mind, if I choose I can catch them up at the post. Where's that waiter gone to? Slow as a funeral they are, these restaurant dinners; I might fix up to have my meals at home; the concierge could do the cooking, and it would be cheaper too. He'd make a mess of it, for a certainty. I'm a fool; deadly dull it would be, and how about the days when I don't come back? At least in a restaurant one isn't bored. What's that waiter up to?

II. Dramatic Monologue

An unintroduced, uninterrupted transcription of what some character situated in a given time and circumstances is saying to some other character, whose responses, if any, are merely reflected in the monologue. The listener is now a separate person but not the reader, who merely overhears. This is inter-personal communication. It creates a double tale: at the same time the monologuist is telling a story he is also enacting one. What he is saying may be no more important than *that* he is saying it now and to this particular person. Such stories feature verbal behavior and self-betrayal of the speaker.

"THE APOSTATE"[2]

By George Milburn

Harry, you been jacking me up about how I been neglecting Rotary here lately, so I'm just going to break down and tell you something. Now I don't want you to take this personal, Harry, because it's not meant personal at all. No siree! Not *a*-tall! But just between you and I, Harry, I'm not going to be coming out to Rotary lunches any more. I mean I'm quitting Rotary! . . .

Now whoa there! Whoa! Whoa just a minute and let me get in a word edgeways. Just let me finish my little say.

Don't you never take it into your head that I haven't been wrestling with this thing plenty. I mean I've argued it all out with myself. Now I'm going to tell you the whyfor and the whereof and the howcome about this, Harry, but kindly don't let what I say go no further. Please keep it strictly on the Q.T. Because I guess the rest of the boys would suspicion that I was turning highbrow on them. But you've always been a buddy to me, Harry, you mangy old son of a hoss thief, you, so what I'm telling you is the straight dope.

Harry, like you no doubt remember, up till a few months ago Rotary was about "the most fondest thing I is of," as the nigger says. There wasn't nothing that stood higher for me than Rotary.

Well, here, about a year ago last fall I took a trip down to the university to visit my son and go to a football game. You know Hubert Junior, my boy. Sure. Well, this is his second year down at the university. Yes, that boy is getting a col-

[2] From *The Apostate*, by George Milburn, copyright 1959, reprinted by permission of Paul R. Reynolds, Inc., 599 Fifth Avenue, New York 17, New York.

lege education. I mean, I'm all for youth having a college education.

Of course, I think there is such a thing as too much education working a detriment. Take, for instance, some of these longhairs running around knocking the country right now. But what I mean is, a good, sound, substantial college education. I don't mean a string of letters a yard long for a man to write after his John Henry. I just mean that I want my boy to have his sheepskin, they call it, before he starts out in the world. Like the fellow says, I want him to get his A.B. degree, and then he can go out and get his J.O.B.

Now, Harry, I always felt like a father has got certain responsibilities to his son. That's just good Rotary. That's all that is. You know that that's just good Rotary yourself, Harry. Well, I always wanted Hubert to think about me just like I was a pal to him, or say an older brother, maybe. Hubert always knew that all he had to do was come to me, and I would act like a big buddy to him, irregardless.

Well, like I was telling you, Harry, I started Hubert in to the university two years ago, and after he had been there about two months, I thought I would run down and see how he was getting along and go to a football game. So I and Mrs. T. drove over one Friday. We didn't know the town very well, so we stopped at a filling station, and I give Hubert a ring, and he come right on down to where we was to show us the way. Just as soon as he come up, I could see right then that he had something on his mind bothering him.

He called me aside and took me into the filling station restroom, and says: "For the love of God, Dad, take that Rotary button out of your coat lapel," he says to me.

III. Letter Narration

The direct presentation of a series of letters written by one character to another; usually a two-way exchange, in which case the letters not only report recent events but may also themselves be, or create, events. Thus, these are also double stories — at once a drama going on now and a narrative of previous action. Letters feature a continually shifting date of narration, so that the correspondent is, until the last letter, always speaking from within the events instead of from the vantage point of their conclusion. One-way correspondence leads to the next group.

CLARISSA

By Samuel Richardson

Miss Clarissa Harlowe to Miss Arabelle Harlowe

Friday, July 21

If, my dearest sister, I did not think the state of my health very precarious, and that it was my duty to take this step, I should hardly have dared to approach you, although but with my pen, after having found your censures so dreadfully justified as they have been.

I have not the courage to write to my father himself, nor yet to my mother. And it is with trembling that I address myself to you, to beg of you to intercede for me, that my father will have the goodness to revoke that heaviest part of the very heavy curse he laid upon me, which relates to HERE-AFTER: for, as to the HERE, *I have indeed met with my punishment from the very wretch in whom I was supposed to place my confidence.*

As I hope not for restoration to favor, I may be allowed to be very earnest on this head: yet will I not use any arguments in support of my request, because I am sure my father, were it in his power, would not have his poor child miserable forever.

I have the most grateful sense of my mother's goodness in sending me up my clothes. I would have acknowledged the favor the moment I received them, with the most thankful duty, but that I feared any line from me would be unacceptable.

I would not give fresh offence: so will decline all other commendations of duty and love; appealing to my heart for both, where *both* are flaming with an ardour that nothing but death can extinguish: therefore only subscribe myself, without so much as a name,

My dear and happy sister,

Your afflicted servant.

IV. Diary Narration

The direct presentation of some character's diary, which of course still features a shifting date of narration; but a diary is addressed neither to a certain person nor to the world at large. It represents a transition between addressing another character and addressing the reader, and hence still purports to be a real-life document. In recording events soon after their occurrence, the narrator is also, intentionally or not, registering his successive states of mind, which also constitute a "story."

THE PASTORAL SYMPHONY[3]

By André Gide

8 May

Dr. Martins came over yesterday from Chaux-de-Fonds. He examined Gertrude's eyes for a long time with the ophthalmoscope. He told me he had spoken about Gertrude to Dr. Roux, the Lausanne specialist, and is to report his observation to him. They both have an idea that Gertrude might be operated on with success. But we have agreed to say nothing to her about it as long as things are not more certain. Martins is to come and let me know what they think after they have consulted. What would be the good of raising Gertrude's hopes if there is any risk of their being immediately extinguished? And besides is she not happy as she is? . . .

10 May

At Easter Jacques and Gertrude saw each other again in my presence — at least Jacques saw Gertrude and spoke to her, but only about trifles. He seemed less agitated than I feared; and I persuaded myself afresh that if his love had really been very ardent, he would not have got over it so easily, even though Gertrude had told him last year before he went away that it was hopeless. I noticed that he no longer says "thou" to Gertrude, but calls her "you" which is certainly preferable; however, I had not asked him to do so and I am

[3] From *Two Symphonies*, trans. Dorothy Bussy (New York: Alfred A. Knopf, 1949), pp. 207–209. Reprinted by permission of the publisher.

glad it was his own idea. There is undoubtedly a great deal of good in him.

I suspect, however, that this submission of Jacque's was not arrived at without a struggle. The unfortunate thing is that the constraint he has been obliged to impose on his feelings now seems good to him in itself; he would like to see it imposed on everyone; I felt this in the discussion I had with him that I have recorded farther back. Is it not La Rochefoucauld who says that the mind is often the dupe of the heart? . . .

V. Subjective Narration

The narrator is the protagonist of his own story, which he is telling to the general public while still at the same age as, or in the same perspective as, when the events of the story ended. He is still under the spell of these events. Although he is writing from the vantage point of the conclusion, his understanding is still limited in some way either by inexperience, native imperception, or participation-blindness. Part of the story is his present distortion of the past events. Also, he is an amateur narrator who speaks *as if* he had a personal audience; he wants to confess to the world, defy it, or justify himself in its eyes. Style is still apt to be vernacular, and the organization distorted by a subjective classification, logic, and rhetoric. This begins the range of merely personal rather than interpersonal communication.

"MY SISTER'S MARRIAGE"[4]

By Cynthia Rich

When my mother died she left just Olive and me to take care of Father. Yesterday when I burned the package of Olive's letters that left only me. I know that you'll side with my sister in all of this because you're only outsiders, and strangers can afford to sympathize with young love, and with whatever sounds daring and romantic, without thinking what

[4] Reprinted from *Mademoiselle;* copyright © 1955 by Street & Smith Publications, Inc., New York. Reprinted by permission of the publisher.

it does to all the other people involved. I don't want you to hate my sister — I don't hate her — but I do want you to see that we're happier this way, Father and I, and as for Olive, she made her choice.

But if you weren't strangers, all of you, I wouldn't be able to tell you about this. "Keep yourself to yourself," my father has always said. "If you ever have worries, Sarah Ann, you come to me and don't go sharing your problems around town." And that's what I've always done. So if I knew you I certainly wouldn't ever tell you about Olive throwing the hairbrush, or about finding the letters buried in the back of the drawer.

I don't know what made Olive the way she is. We grew up together like twins — there were people who thought we were — and every morning before we went to school she plaited my hair and I plaited hers before the same mirror in the same little twist of ribbons and braids behind our heads. We wore the same dresses and there was never a stain on the hem or a rip in our stockings to say to a stranger that we had lost our mother. And although we have never been well-to-do — my father is a doctor and his patients often can't pay — I know that there are people here in Conkling today who think we're rich, just because of little things like candlelight at dinner and my father's cigarette holder and the piano lessons that Olive and I had and the reproduction of "The Anatomy Lesson" that hangs above the mantelpiece instead of botanical prints. "You don't have to be rich to be a gentleman," my father says, "or to live like one."

My father is a gentleman and he raised Olive and myself as ladies. I can hear you laughing, because people like to make fun of words like "gentleman" and "lady," but they are words with ideals and standards behind them, and I hope that I will always hold to those ideals as my father taught me to. If Olive has renounced them, at least we did all we could.

Perhaps the reason that I can't understand Olive is that I have never been in love. I know that if I had ever fallen in love it would not have been, like Olive, at first sight, but only after a long acquaintance. My father knew my mother for seven years before he proposed — it is much the safest way. Nowadays people make fun of that too, and the magazines are full of stories about people meeting in the moonlight and marrying the next morning, but if you read those stories you know that they are not the sort of people you would want to be like.

Even today Olive couldn't deny that we had a happy childhood. She used to be very proud of being the lady of the house, of sitting across the candlelight from my father at dinner like a little wife. Sometimes my father would hold his carving knife poised above the roast to stand smiling at her and say: "Olive, every day you remind me more of your mother."

I think that although she liked the smile, she minded the compliment, because she didn't like to hear about Mother. Once when my father spoke to her she said: "Papa, you're missing Mother again. I can't bear it when you miss Mother. Don't I take care of you all right? Don't I make things happy for you?" It wasn't that she hadn't loved Mother but that she wanted my father to be completely happy.

To tell the truth, it was Olive Father loved best. There was a time when I couldn't have said that, it would have hurt me too much. Taking care of our father was like playing a long game of "let's pretend," and when little girls play family nobody wants to be the children. I thought it wasn't fair, just because Olive was three years older, that she should always be the mother. I wanted to sit opposite my father at dinner and have him smile at me like that.

I was glad when Olive first began walking out with young men in the summer evenings. Then I would make lemonade for my father ("Is it as good as Olive's?") and we would sit out on the screened porch together watching the fireflies. I asked him about the patients he had seen that day, trying to think of questions as intelligent as Olive's. I knew that he was missing her and frowning into the long twilight for the swing of her white skirts. When she came up the steps he said, "I missed my housewife tonight," just as though I hadn't made the lemonade right after all. She knew, too, that it wasn't the same for him in the evenings without her and for a while, instead of going out, she brought the young men to the house. But soon she stopped even that ("I never realized how silly and shallow they were until I saw them with Papa," she said. "I was ashamed to have him talk to them"). I knew that he was glad, and when my turn came I didn't want to go out because I hated leaving them alone together. It all seems a very long time ago. I used to hate it when Olive "mothered" me. Now I feel a little like Olive's mother, and she is like my rebellious child.

In spite of everything, I loved Olive. When we were children we used to play together. The other children disliked us because we talked like grownups and didn't like to get dirty, but we were happy playing by ourselves on the front lawn where my father, if he were home, could watch us from his study window. So it wasn't surprising that when we grew older we were still best friends. I loved Olive and I see now how she took advantage of that love. Sometimes I think she felt that if she was to betray my father she wanted me to betray him too.

VI. Detached Autobiography

Still the protagonist of his own story, the narrator is able to report his experience in a way that squares with the reader's understanding and that calls very little attention to his present self; whatever bias he has he is aware of. Usually he is looking back through a distance of time that permits him to disengage his present self from his former self and to understand now what he did not understand then. As such, the story is about growth and self-knowledge. Effectively if not literally, the speaker and the subject have split in two — into a first and a third person, as speaker and listener split off before. (See II. Dramatic Monologue.) This the distinction between informer and information, the narrating and the narrated, becomes much clearer.

GREAT EXPECTATIONS

By Charles Dickens

At the time when I stood in the churchyard, reading the family tombstones, I had just enough learning to be able to spell them out. My construction even of their simple meaning was not very correct, for I read "wife of the Above" as a complimentary reference to my father's exaltation to a better world; and if any one of my deceased's relations had been referred to as "Below," I have no doubt I should have formed the worst opinions of that member of the family. Neither were my notions of the theological positions to which my Catechism bound me, at all accurate; for, I have a lively remembrance that I supposed my declaration that I was to "walk in the same all the days of my life," laid me under an obligation always to go through the village from our house in one particular direction, and never to vary it by turning down by the wheelwright's or up by the mill.

When I was old enough, I was to be apprenticed to Joe, and until I could assume that dignity I was not to be what Mrs. Joe called "Pompeyed," or (as I render it) pampered. Therefore, I was not only odd-boy about the forge, but if any neighbour happened to want an extra boy to frighten birds, or pick up stones, or do any such job, I was favoured with the employment. In order, however, that our superior position might not be compromised thereby, a money-box was kept on the kitchen mantel-shelf, into which it was publicly made known that all my earnings were dropped. I have an impression that they were to be contributed eventually towards the liquidation of the National Debt, but I know I had no hope of any personal participation in the treasure.

Mr. Wopsle's great-aunt kept an evening school in the village; that is to say, she was a ridiculous old woman of limited means and unlimited infirmity, who used to go to sleep from six to seven every evening, in the society of youth who paid two-pence per week each, for the improving opportunity of seeing her do it. She rented a small cottage, and Mr. Wopsle had the room up-stairs, where we students used to overhear him reading aloud in a most dignified and terrific manner, and occasionally bumping on the ceiling. There was a fiction that Mr. Wopsle "examined" the scholars, once a quarter. What he did on those occasions was to turn up his cuffs, stick up his hair, and give us Mark Antony's oration over the body of Cæsar. This was always followed by Collins's Ode on the Passions, wherein I particularly venerated Mr. Wopsle as Revenge, throwing his bloodstained sword in thunder down, and taking the War denouncing trumpet with a withering look. It was not with me then, as it was in later life, when I fell into the society of the Passions, and compared them with Collins and Wopsle, rather to the disadvantage of both gentlemen.

VII. *Memoir, or Observer Narration*

The narrator tells of what happens essentially to someone else, though he may have been a participator in the action. He identifies himself, states what his relation was to the main character(s) and the events, and expresses his reactions to them. Depending on how close he was to the people and events, he had access to information by three possible channels — confidant, eyewitness, and membership in a community or "chorus." The value of such a narrator is that he can provide an external and at the same time privileged personal view of the protagonist and what happened. The key is often *resonance* between speaker and spoken-about, first and third persons; what happens in the protagonist resounds in the narrator. Though actually two different people, a vicarious relation binds them. This is the frontier between autobiography and biography, first person and third person narrative.

THE GREAT GATSBY[5]

By F. Scott Fitzgerald

I stayed late that night, Gatsby asked me to wait until he was free, and I lingered in the garden until the inevitable swimming party had run up, chilled and exalted, from the black beach, until the lights were extinguished in the guest-rooms overhead. When he came down the steps at last the tanned skin was drawn unusually tight on his face, and his eyes were bright and tired.

"She didn't like it," he said immediately.

"Of course she did."

"She didn't like it," he insisted. "She didn't have a good time."

He was silent, and I guessed at his unutterable depression.

"I feel far away from her," he said. "It's hard to make her understand."

[5] Reprinted with the permission of Charles Scribner's Sons from THE GREAT GATSBY by F. Scott Fitzgerald: Copyright 1925 Charles Scribner's Sons; renewal copyright 1953 Frances Scott Fitzgerald Lanahan; and with the permission of The Bodley Head Ltd. from F. SCOTT FITZGERALD Vol. I.

"You mean about the dance?"

"The dance?" He dismissed all the dances he had given with a snap of his fingers. "Old sport, the dance is unimportant."

He wanted nothing less of Daisy than that she should go to Tom and say: "I never loved you." After she had obliterated four years with that sentence they could decide upon the more practical measures to be taken. One of them was that, after she was free, they were to go back to Louisville and be married from her house — just as if it were five years ago.

"And she doesn't understand," he said. "She used to be able to understand. We'd sit for hours — "

He broke off and began to walk up and down a desolate path of fruit rinds and discarded favors and crushed flowers.

"I wouldn't ask too much of her," I ventured. "You can't repeat the past."

"Can't repeat the past?" he cried incredulously. "Why, of course you can!"

He looked around him wildly, as if the past were lurking here in the shadow of his house, just out of reach of his hand.

"I'm going to fix everything just the way it was before," he said, nodding determinedly. "She'll see."

He talked a lot about the past, and I gathered that he wanted to recover something, some idea of himself perhaps, that had gone into loving Daisy. His life had been confused and disordered since then, but if he could once return to a certain starting place and go over it all slowly, he could find out what that thing was. . . .

One autumn night, five years before, they had been walking down the street when the leaves were falling, and they came to a place where there were no trees and the sidewalk was white with moonlight. They stopped here and turned toward each other. Now it was a cool night with that mysterious excitement in it which comes at the two changes of the year. The quiet lights in the houses were humming out into the darkness and there was a stir and bustle among the stars. Out of the corner of his eye Gatsby saw that the blocks of the sidewalks really formed a ladder and mounted to a secret place above the trees — he could climb to it, if he climbed alone, and once there he could suck on the pap of life, gulp down the incomparable milk of wonder.

His heart beat faster and faster as Daisy's white face came up to his own. He knew that when he kissed this girl, and forever wed his unutterable visions to her perishable breath, his mind would never romp again like the mind of God. So he waited, listening for a moment longer to the tuning-fork that had been struck upon a star. Then he kissed her. At his lips' touch she blossomed for him like a flower and the incarnation was complete.

Through all he said, even through his appalling sentimentality, I was reminded of something — an elusive rhythm, a fragment of lost words that I had heard somewhere a long time ago. For a moment a phrase tried to take shape in my mouth and my lips parted like a dumb man's, as though there was more struggling upon them than a wisp of startled air. But they made no sound, and what I had almost remembered was uncommunicable forever.

VIII. Biography, or Anonymous Narration: Single Character Point of View

This is the beginning of impersonal communication: the narrator (now more nearly the author himself) tells what happens to someone else, but without identifying himself and telling how he knows what he knows. He makes claims, however, to the same three kinds of information that a confidant, eyewitness, and chorus might provide, namely knowledge of the inner life, of immediate action, and of general circumstances and background. Of course, the organization and language are those of the author, not of any character except where quoted, and ultimately the unseen narrator's perspective frames the story. Privy to the character's thought and perceptions as paraphrased by the author, the reader sees the events as both of them see them. Presentation of a *single* character's point of view usually indicates certain themes such as the individual *vs.* society, the confrontation of self and world, or the contrast of private and public reality.

By Herman Melville

Presently the ship's bell sounded two o'clock; and through the cabin-windows a slight rippling of the sea was discerned; and from the desired direction.

"There," exclaimed Captain Delano, "I told you so, Don Benito, look!"

He had risen to his feet, speaking in a very animated tone, with a view the more to rouse his companion. But though the crimson curtain of the stern-window near him that moment fluttered against his pale cheek, Don Benito seemed to have even less welcome for the breeze than the calm.

Poor fellow, thought Captain Delano, bitter experience has taught him that one ripple does not make a wind, any more than one swallow a summer. But he is mistaken for once. I will get his ship in for him, and prove it.

Briefly alluding to his weak condition, he urged his host to remain quietly where he was, since he (Captain Delano) would with pleasure take upon himself the responsibility of making the best use of the wind.

Upon gaining the deck, Captain Delano started at the unexpected figure of Atufal, monumentally fixed at the threshold, like one of those sculptured porters of black marble guarding the porches of Egyptian tombs.

But this time the start was, perhaps, purely physical. Atufal's presence, singularly attesting docility even in sullenness, was contrasted with that of the hatchet-polishers, who in patience evinced their industry; while both spectacles showed, that lax as Don Benito's general authority might be, still, whenever he chose to exert it, no man so savage or colossal but must, more or less, bow.

Snatching a trumpet which hung from the bulwarks, with a free step Captain Delano advanced to the forward edge of the poop, issuing his orders in his best Spanish. The few sailors and many negroes, all equally pleased, obediently set about heading the ship toward the harbour.

While giving some directions about setting a lower stunsail, suddenly Captain Delano heard a voice faithfully repeating his orders. Turning, he saw Babo, now for the time acting, under the pilot, his original part of captain of the slaves. This assistance proved valuable. Tattered sails and warped yards were soon brought into some trim. And no brace or halyard was pulled but to the blithe songs of the inspirited negroes.

Good fellows, thought Captain Delano, a little training would make fine sailors of them. Why see, the very women pull and sing, too. These must be some of those Ashantee negresses that make such capital soldiers, I've heard. But who's at the helm? I must have a good hand there.

He went to see.

IX. *Anonymous Narration:* *Dual Character Point of View*

What applies above (VIII. Biography, or Anonymous Narration: Single Character Point of View) applies here, except that the presentation of *two* characters' inner lives almost certainly announces the different themes of a meeting, conflict, or failure to meet of two people, an ironic discrepancy between their perspectives, or a dual character sketch. Also, the total effect is usually a greater impartiality on the part of the narrator.

"UNLIGHTED LAMPS"[6]

By Sherwood Anderson

The farmer hitched his horse and brought it to the door and the doctor drove off feeling strangely weak and at the same time strong. How simple now seemed the thing he had yet to do. Perhaps when he got home his daughter would have gone to bed but he would ask her to get up and come into the office. Then he would tell the whole story of his marriage and its failure sparing himself no humiliation. "There was something very dear and beautiful in my Ellen and I must make Mary understand that. It will help her to be a beautiful woman," he thought, full of confidence in the strength of his resolution.

[6] Reprinted by permission of Harold Ober Associates, Inc. Copyright 1921 by B. W. Huebsch. Renewed 1948 by Eleanor Copenhaver Anderson.

He got to the door of the livery barn at eleven o'clock and Barney Smithfield with young Duke Yetter and two other men sat talking here. The liveryman took his horse away into the darkness of the barn and the doctor stood for a moment leaning against the wall of the building. The town's night watchman stood with the group by the barn door and a quarrel broke out between him and Duke Yetter, but the doctor did not hear the hot words that flew back and forth or Duke's loud laughter at the night watchman's anger. A queer hesitating mood had taken possession of him. There was something he passionately desired to do but could not remember. Did it have to do with his wife Ellen or Mary his daughter? The figures of the two women were again confused in his mind and to add to the confusion there was a third figure, that of the woman he had just assisted through child birth. Everything was confusion. He started across the street toward the entrance of the stairway leading to his office and then stopped in the road and stared about. Barney Smithfield having returned from putting his horse in the stall shut the door of the barn and a hanging lantern over the door swung back and forth. It threw grotesque dancing shadows down over the faces and forms of the men standing and quarreling beside the wall of the barn.

Mary sat by a window in the doctor's office awaiting his return. So absorbed was she in her own thoughts that she was unconscious of the voice of Duke Yetter talking with the men in the street.

When Duke had come into the street the hot anger of the early part of the evening had returned and she again saw him advancing toward her in the orchard with the look of arrogant male confidence in his eyes but presently she forgot him and thought only of her father. An incident of her childhood returned to haunt her. One afternoon in the month of May when she was fiften her father had asked her to accompany him on an evening drive into the country. The doctor went to visit a sick woman at a farmhouse five miles from town and as there had been a great deal of rain the roads were heavy. It was dark when they reached the farmer's house and they went into the kitchen and ate cold food off a kitchen table. For some reason her father had, on that evening, appeared boyish and almost gay. On the road he had talked a little. Even at that early age Mary had grown tall and her figure was becoming womanly. After the cold supper in the farm kitchen he walked with her around the house and she sat on a narrow porch. For a moment her father stood before her. He put his hands into his trouser pockets and throwing back his head laughed most heartily. "It seems strange to think you will soon be a woman," he said. "When you do become a woman what do you suppose is going to happen, eh? What kind of a life will you lead? What will happen to you?"

The doctor sat on the porch beside the child and for a moment she had thought he was about to put his arm around her. Then he jumped up and went into the house leaving her to sit alone in the darkness.

X. *Anonymous Narration:*
Multiple Character Point of View

Going into the minds of several or many characters builds up a panoramic cross-reference of perspectives and is used to explore thoroughly a group, community, society, or epoch. The concern is communal, and the result is a broad impersonal perspective created by the characters but beyond any one of them. The author may retire and let the characters play confidant, eyewitness, and chorus to each other. The old personal tie between narrator and protagonist is broken down even further.

SHIP OF FOOLS[7]

By Katherine Anne Porter

Earlier in that evening at dinner, Herr Professor Hutten, still lacking his proper appetite, barely refrained from pushing away his loaded plate, rising and seeking fresh air; but his wife was eating well, and though the sight was faintly repugnant to him, still there was no good reason for interrupting her. The other guests seemed as usual, the Doctor amiably silent, Herr Rieber and Fräulein Lizzi exuding their odious atmosphere of illicit intimacy, Frau Schmitt unremarkable as ever; only Frau Rittersdorf was chatting away lightly in the direction of the Captain — a frivolous woman, with what a vanity at her age! — and even if Herr Professor Hutten had no hope of hearing anything in the least edifying or enlightening, he listened in the wan hope of some distraction from his inner unease.

Frau Rittersdorf noted his attention, saw the other faces beginning to take on a listening look; without loosing her hold on the attention of Captain Thiele, she turned clever glances upon the others and raised her voice a little to include them in the circle of those who had been lately amused or annoyed or both with the antic of the zarzuela company and their *outré* notions of the etiquette of social occasions on shipboard — if such a word could be used even remotely in such a connection. There was above all that impudent creature they called Tito, who had tried to sell her some tickets of one kind or another for some sort of petty cheat they had thought up among themselves, who knew what?

"Ah yes," Lizzi broke in, "for a raffle! I bought one and got rid of them."

"You should have told me!" cried Herr Rieber. "For I bought *two* — you must give one of yours away!"

"I'll return it to them and get back my money!" whinnied Lizzi, tossing her head.

"Oh," said Frau Rittersdorf, "that should be something to see, anyone getting back a pfenning from those bandits, for I know they are that! No, dear Fraulein, good businesswoman, that you are, everyone knows, but you will want to be better than that!"

"But wonderful dancing partners, don't you find, Frau Rittersdorf?" asked Herr Rieber, gleefully. Lizzi slapped his hand, annoyed, because she had meant to say that herself. "Shame on you," she said, "you are not very kind. Dancing partners are sometimes scarce, one cannot always choose too delicately."

Frau Rittersdorf, shocked at this turn of talk just when she was ready to give a sparkling account of that unusual incident, cried out in a high yet ladylike soprano, "Ah, but there are effronteries so utterly unexpected one is taken off guard, one is defenseless, it is better to follow one's instinct — yes, as well as training! and to behave as if nothing out of the way were happening — how could I dream of such a thing as that?" She sat back and held her napkin to her lips, staring over it in distress at Lizzi, whose laugh was a long cascade of falling tinware.

"Ah, but that is just what ladies are supposed to dream about," called Herr Rieber in delight, leaning forward to make himself heard over Lizzi's clamor. "What is wrong with that, please tell me?"

Pig-dog, thought Frau Rittersdorf, her dismay turning in a flash to a luxury of rage, at least I am not reduced to dancing with you! She bared her teeth at him and lifted her brows and narrowed her eyes: 'Are you sure you would know what *ladies* dream about, Herr Rieber?" she inquired, dangerously.

These tactics impressed Herr Rieber, who had got his face smacked more than once by easily offended ladies, and at that moment Frau Rittersdorf resembled every one of them, in tone and manner. A man couldn't be too cautious with that proper, constipated type, no matter how gamey she looked. He wilted instantly, unconditionally.

XI. *Anonymous Narration:*
No Character Point of View

In withdrawing from the minds of all his characters, the author reduces his roles as informer to two — eyewitness and chorus. He no longer plays confidant to anyone. One result is something like legend or myth, where external deeds and words carry the story by themselves with the narrator supplying background information and commentary. The characters tend to be typical or universal, the action symbolic or ritualistic. Personal psychology is not the point. These are thoroughly communal stories with an archetypal psychology. Another result is the external sketch. The next step would be to drop the eyewitness role as well, leaving only chorus information in the form of generalized chronicles, digests of the sorts of documents covered up to here. In other words, the rest is history, summaries of summaries of summaries.

By Nathaniel Hawthorne

The next day, the whole village of Milford talked of little else than Parson Hooper's black veil. That, and the mystery concealed behind it, supplied a topic for discussion between acquaintances meeting in the street, and good women gossiping at their open windows. It was the first item of news that the tavern-keeper told to his guests. The children babbled of it on their way to school. One imitative little imp covered his face with an old black handkerchief, thereby so affrighting his playmates that the panic seized himself, and he wellnigh lost his wits by his own waggery.

It was remarkable that of all the busybodies and impertinent people in the parish, not one ventured to put the plain question to Mr. Hooper, wherefore he did this thing. Hitherto, whenever there appeared the slightest call for such interference, he had never lacked advisers, nor shown himself averse to be guided by their judgment. If he erred at all, it was by so painful a degree of self-distrust, that even the mildest censure would lead him to consider an indifferent action as a crime. Yet, though so well acquainted with this amiable weakness, no individual among his parishioners chose to make the black veil a subject of friendly remonstrance. There was a feeling of dread, neither plainly confessed nor carefully concealed, which caused each to shift the responsibility upon another, till at length it was found expedient to send a deputation of the church, in order to deal with Mr. Hooper about the mystery, before it should grow into a scandal. Never did an embassy so ill discharge its duties. The minister received them with friendly courtesy, but became silent, after they were seated, leaving to his visitors the whole burden of introducing their important business. The topic, it might be supposed, was obvious enough. There was the black veil swathed round Mr. Hooper's forehead, and concealing every feature above his placid mouth, on which, at times, they could per-

ceive the glimmering of a melancholy smile. But that piece of
crape, to their imagination, seemed to hang down before his
heart, the symbol of a fearful secret between him and them.
Were the veil but cast aside, they might speak freely of it, but
not till then. Thus they sat a considerable time, speechless,
confused, and shrinking uneasily from Mr. Hooper's eye,
which they felt to be fixed upon them with an invisible
glance. Finally, the deputies returned abashed to their constituents, pronouncing the matter too weighty to be handled,
except by a council of the churches, if, indeed, it might not
require a general synod.

Techniques of Fiction

Ever since Henry James established the concept of a central
intelligence or authority through whom the experience of the
story is filtered to the reader, discussions of point of view have
recognized four or five techniques — so-called omniscient third-
person, third-person limited to one character's point of view,
retrospective autobiography, first-person observer narration, and
sometimes a subjective or unreliable narration.

In an incomplete theory, these categories seemed to be based
on mixed principles — on distinctions, for example, between
whether the character or the author is filtering the experience,
whether the narrator is his own protagonist or focusing on another, and whether his account is reliable or not. Besides omit-
ting other important distinctions, this classification can lead to
a great deal of confusion. Some "omniscience" is more omniscient than others, and no third-person narration can really be
limited to the point of view of a character. And while recognized as techniques in some contexts, interior and dramatic
monologues, letters, and diaries never seem to get integrated
into considerations of point of view. Many stories are indis-
criminately called "monologues" in one discussion and indis-
criminately described as first-person or subjective in another.
Finally, so long as all the techniques are not placed in relation
one to another, they suggest no sequence — a loss not only for
teachers and literary critics but also for any reader interested in

the connections between form and content, or narrative art and everyday expression. This chapter attempts to contribute a comprehensive, unifying theory of narrative.

The techniques of fiction imitate everyday recording and reporting. The stories in the first two groups (interior monologue, dramatic monologue) purport to be actual discourse going on "now" — somebody thinking, somebody speaking. The stories of the next five groups purport to be documents written by characters in the story — letters, diaries, autobiographies, or memoirs. What we are asked to believe about all of the remaining stories, of course, is that the events really happened and that therefore these (third-person) narratives are also actual documents — biographies, case histories, or chronicles. Of course art implies artifice; my reader can note for himself what the differences are between these fictional forms and their real-life counterparts.

Any piece of fiction one might name falls somewhere along the spectrum, or represents some combination of the techniques illustrated herein. Familiarity with the storyteller's full repertory makes a particular author's choice of form more meaningful. You cannot separate the tale from the telling. Beneath the content of every message is intent. And form embodies that intent. Intuitively or not, an author chooses his techniques according to his meaning. Spontaneous attention to form will tell the reader more about what the author is doing and what he means than a direct analysis of meaning will do — besides preserving his pleasure. To appreciate the connection between form and subject, just imagine *Vanity Fair* told by one of its characters instead of by the godlike author, or *The Great Gatsby* narrated by Gatsby instead of Nick, or *Great Expectations* told by an anonymous narrator who enters the minds of all the characters, instead of by Pip. Changes in intent, effect, meaning, and theme occur as the technique shifts in the foregoing samples.

Because they feature unreliable or fallible speakers, the stories in the first five groups force us to pay attention to motive and attitude and style and tone, to all those qualities of the speaker and his language that come through easily in everyday conversation but that become subtler on the page, especially in the techniques of anonymous narration that appear later in the spectrum. Third-person stories look deceptively bland: the speaker is hidden, we take his guidance for granted, and easily forget that — "third-person" or not — this story is being told by *somebody* and that that somebody exerts a rhetoric just as individual and influential as that of any character *I*.

Every story is first-person, whether the speaker identifies himself or not. Interior monologues, dramatic monologues, letters, diaries, and subjective narrations keep alive the drama of the narrating act: they put the speaker on display, so that we cannot ignore or forget the way he talks, the kind of logic he uses, and the organization he imposes on experience. Although Mark Twain tells the story of Tom Sawyer himself, instead of talking through Huck, as he does in *Huckleberry Finn,* he has ways of organizing and setting down his material just as unique as Huck's. And the authors Goethe and Samuel Richardson are essentially in the same position when they write, as Goethe's young Werther is when recording his sorrows in his diary, or Richardson's Clarissa Harlowe is when putting down in letters her plans to avert seduction. The difference is that the monologues of Huck, Werther, and Clarissa are spontaneous, vernacular, and private, whereas the monologues of Twain, Goethe and Richardson are composed, literary, and public. After listening to the everyday voices of characters caught in the open with all their prejudices showing, it is easier to detect and appreciate the subtleties of the detached professional writer. As Walker Gibson puts it in talking of "the speaking voice" in fiction, "We all play roles, all the time. I don't mean this is dishonesty — it is simply a way we have of making ourselves understood." This is no less true of the professional author than of Tom, Dick, or Harry. "To write a composition," says Gibson, "is to decide three things . . . who you are; what your situation is (your 'subject'); who your audience is." The key word is *composition*. When Tom speaks or writes spontaneously to Dick, he makes the above decisions more or less unconsciously; when we behave like an author, we pay more attention to such decisions. When we act as a reader, we need to know how such decisions are made.

There is another way in which the earlier techniques prepare for the later ones. Interior and dramatic monologues, letters, diaries, and personal documents are some of the building blocks of the larger, less limited techniques. Most novels contain some directly quoted thoughts and dialogue. And many novels, like Lawrence Durrell's *Alexandria Quartet,* incorporate the texts of letters and diaries. *Moby Dick* touches every part of the spectrum; there are the soliloquies of Ahab, dramatic monologue and dialogue, autobiography and observer narration by Ishmael, and broad, anonymous narration set by the author. A reader familiar with stories consisting entirely of monologue or document (letters, diary) is at a great advantage when plunged into the hubbub of voices that makes up the conventional novel or short story purporting to be memoir, biography, or chronicle.

More generally, each technique in this spectrum, regarded as real-life reportage, is more comprehensive and abstract, takes in more territory, than the ones before it. This comes from the narrator's increasingly complicated job of compiling and assimilating material from more and more remote sources — of incorporating and digesting, quoting and paraphrasing. A social worker would have to summarize much more material to tell the story of a client or group of clients than one of these clients would have to for his own diary or for an impromptu monologue. Throughout the spectrum, the narrator of the story becomes less and less confined to a particular time and place of telling and being listened to, and farther and farther removed from the time and place of the events narrated. He floats more and more freely, regardless of the concreteness of his language, and his broadening vantage point implies greater and greater selection and reorganization of his original information; at the same time, his more public audience demands of him a more universal style, rhetoric, and logic.

The Learning Process

The narrative sequence corresponds closely to Piaget's description of the evolution of learning in the child. What hinders the growth of understanding, he says, is an unconscious preference for a limited local point of view. Learning is a matter of "decentering," of breaking through our egocentricity to new points of view not determined solely by our physical vantage point in time and space or by our emotional preferences. We achieve decentering by adapting ourselves to things and people outside ourselves and by adopting points of view initially foreign to us, as the anonymous narrator does with his single, dual, and multiple character points of view. This amounts to expanding one's perspective; one does not become less egocentric, but his center becomes an area, not just a point. In the last group of stories, the narrator is centered in the middle of the community consciousness.

If we imagine something called a primary moment of experience, such as what an interior monologue records on the spot, we may think of the other sections of the spectrum as stages in the processing of this experience, as ways of combining it with other experiences, as forms in which it is talked about, levels to which it is abstracted, and vantage points from which it is viewed. These are all different ways of expressing decentering and may demonstrate how this difficult and lifelong learning comes about. It makes a difference whether the moment of primary experience has just happened or happened a long time ago, whether it has happened to the speaker or someone else, and whether he is confiding it to an acquaintance or broadcasting it to a larger audience. The stories at the end of the spectrum are not, of course, superior to the earlier ones. What is important are the different modes of abstracting experience and what they correspond to in real life.

To speak of the reader's learning process, it seems that, ideally, comprehension and appreciation should happen, and happen as one reads, without formal analysis. Intuitions are swift and deep, and intuitions can be developed. A course of reading that is structured according to some fundamental relations has advantages: the reader gains a perspective of the woods as he moves among the trees, and the spectacle of gradually shifting shapes permits him to grasp the facts about the field intuitively by himself. Real learning is not accepting statements of the sort made in this essay but reorganizing constantly one's own inner field in an effort to match it with the field of study. Stories may magnetize each other if they are sequenced so as to exploit the basic structure of discourse.

The interrelation of life and literature is both more precise and more organic than is commonly expressed in the truism that one can learn one through the other. Fiction holds a mirror up not only to our other behavior but to our modes of communicating and learning. It does this not only in what it says but in how it says it. By moving freely back and forth among the three realms of fiction, discourse, and growth, via a common concept, we can bring them to bear on each other and thus understand each better. The very subject matter of fiction inevitably concerns the making and breaking of communication among people, someone's learning or failure to learn, or something about discrepancies and adjustments of perspective. We invite the reader to test this statement with any story that comes to mind. Stories both *are* systems of communication and knowledge, and *are about* such systems. Good art, as we all know, weds form to content, either through the dissonance of irony or the consonance of harmony. What makes such fusions possible is that our ways of apprehending and sharing experience are themselves a crucial part of what we call experience.

Uses of the Spectrum

First, a few suggestions that do not directly concern the classroom.

Perhaps this schema could be of use to critics and reviewers, who could in turn help, more than they sometimes do, the average reader. Most of us are content-bound by training. We ask ourselves unnecessarily complicated questions about what a story means and what the author is doing, when a simple glance at the communication structure of the work would answer many of these questions. Every message has intent as well as content, and form embodies this intent. Gatsby is "great" only as seen by Nick; if you want to create a semi-legendary figure of romantic mystery you do not take the reader into his mind. And can you imagine what would happen to our ship of fools if it were viewed only by one of the characters?

For literary scholars and historians the spectrum might be a revealing way to examine individual authors or epochs or national trends. Some writers, such as Thackeray and Tolstoi, seldom move outside a certain range of the spectrum, whereas others, such as Dostoevski, play it freely from one end to the other. Why has the diary technique been used most, and most successfully, by the French? Why have the British, until very recently, stayed in the third-person range more than the Americans, French, or Russians? Why has the historical development of storytelling followed the reverse of this spectrum, moving from the most abstract and external to the most immediate and internal?

Generally, all people whose work requires writing narrative of some kind, or sifting other people's narratives, should become sophisticated about the relations of lower-order reportage to high-order reportage. An historian or case-writer or lawyer or foreign service officer should ask himself which form squares best with his relations to his material and to his audience. If information is firsthand, to what extent am I an eyewitness or confidant or member of a chorus? Am I playing all the roles I should? In the best ratio? Should I go and look, go and interview, go and ask? If secondhand, what about sources? Are they not precisely such things as recorded interior and dramatic monologues, letters, journals, varied first-person accounts? In *The Use of Personal Documents in the Psychological Sciences,*[8] Gordon Allport has discussed the difficulty of honestly and sen-

[8] New York: Social Science Research Council, 1942.

sitively converting first-person material into third-person when writing up cases. When and how do we quote, summarize, and synthesize these personal documents? Such are the problems of the biographer, historian, and sociologist, who may not, like the novelist, imagine what they do not know. At every stage of abstracting *from* his material and *for* his audience the teller of true tales faces choices involving increasing inference, increasing risk of confusing teller and told.

As regards classroom education itself, the spectrum may be of use, first of all, to the teacher, for whom it is intended to be an aid in understanding narrative technique in terms of abstraction, person, and point of view. What are all the story types and how do they relate to each other? Traditionally, the approach to fiction has been dominated by the Aristotelian categories of plot, character, setting, and theme. Now, for one thing, it is terribly hard to "factor out" these elements in a given story, because they are so interwoven with each other, and it is not at all clear why readers should attempt to do so. Second, since presumably all stories contain all elements, these categories do not enable one to distinguish among story types but only to "analyze" a single story, although some pedagogues and anthologists have attempted, with alarming results, to classify stories according to which element was emphasized. Third, like Aristotle's other theories of language and poetics, the conception of story elements was not created for teaching purposes; it is not part of a pedagogical scheme of discourse. And finally, plot, character, setting, and theme involve issues of who, what, where, when, and why that are best understood by grasping the information and communication systems of a story, and by perceiving how these shift from one story to another.

As a curriculum sequence the narrative spectrum should be used with a strong regard for the maturity of the students at hand and for the different learning problems of reading and writing. For students in elementary school and junior high, the spectrum may provide a sound reading progression *if reversed*. Although this reversed order does roughly recapitulate literary history, I would not of course recommend it for that reason but rather for the reason I mentioned in connection with Northrop Frye's theory of heroes — that child development does in some ways seem to concur with historical development. I said then that children want first to read about the grandiose and the far-fetched — superhuman figures set in the there-then — and that they only gradually come to accept scaled-down characters and everyday situations. As the *Open Court Readers* have put it, very young readers want their heroes to be extreme — much better or much worse than they are themselves. An important correlation exists, I believe, between kinds of heroes and narrative method. It is interesting, for example, that folk and fairy tales, myths, legends, and fables — the stories that contain superhuman or miraculous heroes — are told by an anonymous narrator to an anonymous audience and include little character point of view, if any. The distances between speaker, subject, and listener are at the maximum possible for narratives still featuring individuals. Such stories are impersonal in every sense except for there being heroes at all. When referred to, the inner life of the hero is simply and factually stated, being usually so universal that it need not be presented. Indeed, the main point about archetypal heroes is that they stand for the reader's own psychic content and invite projection by remaining empty. At the other end of the spectrum, the anti-hero, the ironic man who is less than man, appears in conjunction with personal narration of a claustrophobic point of view — the subjective narration of *Notes from Underground,* diaries, interior monologue. The anti-hero speaks for himself, which is to say he hangs himself, and his self-told story is displayed for mockery. It is as if grandeur were a factor of distance! At any rate, judging from children's and adolescents' tastes, it seems that an appropriate progression of fiction reading would lead at once down the scale of heroes and down the scale of abstraction. I hypothesize that both run from *he* to *I,* in some manner that approximates in more or less detail the gradations of the narrative spectrum.

Likewise, the youngest student is apt to cast his own fictions into remote third person, and only gradually differentiate story technique into the many narrator-character-audience relations that I have arrayed. But at this point we have to distinguish between his writing of fiction and his writing of actuality. To the extent that narrative assignments ask him to recount incidents from his own experience, he is perfectly capable of narrating in the first person, and indeed must do so until he has learned to gather the kind of data required for telling what happened to other people. In other words, if the spectrum is to serve as some sort of curriculum guide, it should probably be reversed when the events are being made up but followed as presented here when the events are real. This is in line with the principle, discussed in Chapter Two, that fictionalizing and reporting are different modes of abstracting entailing different psychological processes. If, as I would recommend, a reportage assignment stipulates, not the content, but the writer's relations to his subject and audience, then the student is automatically placed in the position of a narrator of one of the story types on the spectrum. When inventing a story, however, he must *choose* the technique, which, for one thing, presupposes familiarity with all the possibilities, but which also, and more importantly, involves him in the psychic objectification of feeling. In this case, I maintain, the younger he is, the more likely that he will choose a third-person technique. My own proposals for narrative assignments (in *A Student-Centered Language Arts Curriculum*) often leave the order open to further experimentation, but I have suggested that the writing of letters, diaries, and general autobiography begin in elementary school and be followed in junior high by narrative that specializes successively in memoir, biography, and chronicle. Since interior and dramatic monologues are natural discourses anyway, these are not assigned until junior high, when students can become aware of them enough to simulate them fictionally in dramatic activity and in writing.

Senior high and college students who have already encountered most of the narrative spectrum, partly through reading and partly through writing, perhaps piecemeal, perhaps in a limited order, would probably benefit from a sequence of fiction

CHAPTER FIVE

Grammar and the Sentence

So far, we have moved from a general concept of discourse to the spectrum of discourse and thence to two particular kinds of discourse — drama and narrative. Now I would like to magnify that substructure of discourse called syntax, bring into close ken the domain staked out by linguists and described by grammar — the sentence. First, I want to examine the assumption that a knowledge of grammar will improve writing. In Chapter Three I proposed a dialogical approach to sentence development that exploited the processes of expatiation and emendation characteristic of discussion. Part of what follows here is a consideration of the conventional teaching approach that was rejected in that chapter. But there are other ways in which formal sentence analysis, especially that of linguistics, is influencing education. A look at grammar teaching will eventually lead us to those other matters.

Probably no other area of the language arts except beginning reading is so bedevilled with semantic confusion as grammar teaching. What *kind of knowledge* of grammar does one mean

— a working knowledge or a conceptual grasp of grammatical generalizations? What *kind of grammar* — prescriptive or descriptive, a body of rules for correct usage in the standard dialect, or a systematic schematization of syntactic relations? If descriptive, a classificatory, structural, or generative grammar? What *kind of instruction* — identifying parts of speech, filling in blanks with the correct linguistic form, parsing and diagramming sentence examples, making up sentences on a grammatical paradigm or pattern, memorizing concepts and codifications about the operations of syntax? And finally, *improvement in what aspect of writing* — the "mechanics" of punctuation and capitalization, the correction of *me and him went to town,* the expansion of the syntactic repertory in the direction of elaboration and diversification of sentence constructions, or the development of judgment in sentence construction as measured by communicative effectiveness and rhetorical advantage?

What have been the main claims for grammar teaching as regards composition? What improvement in writing have teachers hoped to achieve by such instruction? The claims are of essentially two very different sorts. One concerns correct usage — avoidance of error, or the use of what is generally known as "good grammar." As most linguists tend to conclude nowadays, correctness really means conformity to the particular grammar of standard dialect. In a very meaningful sense, people speak and write incorrectly only when they deviate from the regular practices of the speech community from which they learned their dialect. Inasmuch as *ain't* and *he go now* represent consistent usage in some dialects, they are incorrect only in relation to the norms of standard dialect. In other words, learning to write "correctly" involves a shift of dialect and hence the very sensitive moral and psychological matter of *joining a new speech communty,* that is, the speech community in which standard dialect is preferred.

In this view, teaching a prescriptive body of rules designed to induce correctness appears blandly technical and humanly naive. The student is being asked, in effect, to prefer the dialect of a speech community to which he does not belong and to disavow, in some measure, the way of talking that he learned from his parents and from other people upon whom his sense of personal and social identity depends. A lot more than variation in linguistic forms is entailed in this sort of correction. If school populations, for example, are racially and socio-economically segregated — whether on principle or de facto, by a tracking system — corrective grammar teaching assumes that a speaker of the non-standard dialect should write in standard English even though he is barred from association with speakers of standard English. Actually, to preserve his own sense of integrity, he has a powerful motive not to adopt this alien grammar. It is partly for these reasons that I advocated, in Chapter Three, the heterogeneous mixing of students in the English class and the naturalistic modification of grammar through vocal exchange among these mixed students.

In view of the stand on racial segregation taken in some regions, and of the socio-economic split between urban, suburban, and rural populations all over the country, this proposal no doubt appears very idealistic. But it is precisely at this point in considering corrective grammar teaching that one realizes how much the tradition in which it thrives is a factor of the material facts of life in America. In Washington, D.C., for example, where the school population is rapidly becoming 100% black, the Center for Applied Linguistics has arrived at the following pedagogical strategy. Linguists expert in dialectology are to describe precisely those differences in usage that distinguish the dialects of that population from standard dialect. Then educators are to "develop materials" that will enable students to bridge the gap. Instructional techniques would presumably consist of pattern practice of the sort employed in second-language learning whereby students drill specifically on those points of divergence that constitute errors. Although those dialectologists are more sensitive than anyone to the social and psychological implications of membership in speech communities, and most cognizant of the effective equality of dialects, they have nevertheless settled on a solution that ignores these implications and this equality. They have done so for humane reasons of social engineering: "bad grammar" brands the speaker and bars him from jobs and status.

This strategy and this goal have ever been part and parcel of corrective grammar teaching. The ironic result of this short-sighted "practical" concession to the social facts of life in America is that it bolsters segregation and homogenization of classes and thus defeats its own humane purpose at the same time that it defers a more fundamental solution. So long as we admit — as we certainly should — that corrective grammar is a factor of social engineering, then other alternatives are possible — the re-gerrymandering of school districts throughout a metropolitan area, consolidation of rural schools, the abolition within a school of achievement and ability grouping, and the classroom exploitation of vocal interaction. In short, if standard English grammar, as a behavior, is considered desirable, then let "disadvantaged" students speak with those who use the standard dialect. They will learn it the same way they learned their local dialect, and for the same reason — that they are members of a speech community where it is native.

For most middle-class students reared where standard English is spoken, "errors" are a problem only to the extent that the adult community commits them also, in which case, as in the notorious matter of *as* and *like,* the educator must ask himself what indeed he means by "standard." The individual deviations such as small children make (*I bringed it*) inevitably disappear without correction because in time a child always comes to regularize his speech according to the norms he infers from speech experience.

But let's look more closely at the kinds of errors made by children in both lower and higher socio-economic groups. From everyday experience, anyone can establish the fact that even a first-grader, from whatever language environment, never commits certain syntactic mistakes unless he is aphasic or a foreigner just learning English. No such child ever puts a nominal direct object between subject and predicate (*I the car saw*) or a determiner after the adjective (*Red my hat*). From various research studies it is also clear that by at least fourth grade children use *in their writing* all the kernel-sentence types, all the simple sentence transformations, and all the transformations that operate on embedded sentences. Orally, most children seem to be able to use all the transformations before they enter school. By utterly naturalistic means — conversation, mainly — they have generalized for themselves, in an operational and behavioral way, the regularities of syntax, and constructed some kind of internal model by means of which they can endlessly generate well formed sentences that they have never heard before.

In a longitudinal study of 338 children from whom oral speech samples were elicited at intervals between kindergarten and twelfth grade, Walter Loban found the following problems among the speakers of standard dialect (through ninth grade):[1]

> For those children not handicapped by social dialect, most difficulties fall into five categories, occurring in the following order of frequency:
>
> > inconsistency in the use of tense
> > careless omission of words (excluding omission of auxiliaries)
> > lack of syntactic clarity
> > > ambiguous placement of words, phrases, and clauses
> > > awkward and incoherent arrangements of expression
> > confusing use of pronouns
> > trouble with agreement of subject and verb when using *there is, there are, there was,* and *there were*
>
> It is immediately apparent that all these problems transcend usage. They are matters of sensitivity to clarity and precision of communication. This is not at all what the researcher had expected. (p. 47)

For these "problems that transcend usage," I would add, the writing-workshop approach to composition provides precisely what is needed.

[1] *Problems in Oral Language* (Champaign, Ill.: National Council of Teachers of English, 1966).

What does Loban conclude are the oral language problems of children speaking a "social class dialect"?

Their difficulties fall into ten categories in the following order of frequency:

> lack of agreement of subject and verb, third person singular (other than the forms of the verb *to be*)
>
> omission of auxiliary verbs (especially those formed with the verb *to be*)
>
> inconsistency in the use of tense
>
> nonstandard use of verb forms
>
> lack of agreement of subject and verb while using forms of the verb *to be*
>
> careless omission of words (excluding omission of auxiliaries)
>
> nonstandard use of pronouns
>
> nonstandard use of noun forms
>
> double negatives
>
> omission of the verb *to be* (p. 49)

These errors are confined almost entirely to the forms and inflections of individual words, especially verbs, and more especially the verb *to be*. Though most are errors of usage, none concern sentence construction. Neither group of children showed difficulty connecting with prepositions and conjunctions or modifying with adjectives and adverbs. Both groups had problems with clarity and coherence, as described above.

The gist of all this is that many children do not deviate from standard grammar and that even those who deviate do so in far less significant ways than has been supposed, however conspicuous or nerve-shattering the faults may seem to the sensibilities of English teachers. Speaking generally of the language of elementary school children, Loban reports that there is no significant difference in the structural patterns of high and low proficiency groups (which roughly correspond to higher and lower social classes), but that the higher group shows greater dexterity in using elements within these structures. Where there are subject nominals, for example, the higher group uses clauses, infinitives, and gerundives — not just nouns and pronouns; they have a greater repertory of clauses; they shift movable elements with greater ease. "Not pattern but what is done to achieve flexibility within the pattern proves to be a measure of effectiveness and control of language at this level of language development."[2] This statement is illustrated in the following passage and linked to the findings of a British researcher:

> The research of Basil Bernstein in England and my own research on language development are pertinent here. The Cockney and the upper-middle-class British speaker have the same basic language, the same grammar. The difference lies, according to Bernstein,[3] in the extent to which Cockney fails to use the potential of the language. This is exactly what I found in my research in the Oakland, California, schools. In kindergarten and in subsequent years, the same grammar operates in the language of all the youngsters. But subjects from the lower socio-economic groups do not use the language with as full a range of potential as those from more favored groups. They can use the full potential, but if they are in the lower socio-economic group they do not do so very often. By full potential, I mean using such syntactical devices as coordination or subordination to express a complex idea or using an appositive to reinforce or to extend the listener's understanding of what is being communicated. They do not use infinitives — not so much the infinitive alone as the infinitive phrase, the elaborated infinitive phrase, a much neater device than dependent, subordinate clauses for tightly coiling ideas. Gerund phrases, participial phrases, and infinitive phrases are usually indicative of a much tighter kind of thinking than is the long dependent clause.[4]

Loban's findings are partly corroborated but also possibly somewhat contradicted by the research of Harry Osser[5] and

[2] Walter Loban, *The Language of Elementary School Children* (Champaign, Ill.: National Council of Teachers of English, 1963), p. 84.

[3] Basil Bernstein, "Language and Social Class," *British Journal of Sociology*, XI (1960), 271–276.

[4] "A Sustained Program of Language Learning," *Language Programs for the Disadvantaged* (Champaign, Ill.: National Council of Teachers of English, 1963), pp. 222–223.

[5] "A Study of the Communicative Abilities of Disadvantaged Children," unpublished final report for Office of Economic Opportunity contract no. 2402, 1968.

Arthur McCaffrey.[6] In Osser's research, lower-class Negro pre-schoolers showed less control over thirteen common syntactic structures in standard English, on imitation and comprehension tasks, than middle-class whites, even when efforts were made to compensate for dialectical differences. In McCaffrey's on-going research with pre-schoolers, first-graders, and fifth-graders, the children of lower socioeconomic status likewise performed less well on imitation, comprehension, and production tasks involving thirteen similar syntactic structures. But McCaffrey raises several unsolved problems about what these children's lower scores mean. The Osser-McCaffrey studies are not easily compared with Loban's study, and Loban's somewhat imprecise use of "patterns," furthermore, would introduce ambiguity into any such comparison.

Loban, incidentally, believes grammar instruction to be ineffectual and recommends oral practice and grappling with language problems in real communication situations.[7]

The effort to pinpoint so-called grammatical problems in sentence production inevitably leads us back to the other hope held by proponents of grammar teaching — that a knowledge of grammar will increase the student's syntactic versatility, that is, will enable him to elaborate and diversify his sentence constructions. In writing itself, evidence demonstrates very clearly that children's sentences grow in precisely this direction as a matter of normal development. That elaboration and complexity are developmental seems to be a well established fact. But certain construction feats in particular have been identified by Kellogg Hunt as indices of syntactic growth.[8] They are: (1) the increasing modification of nouns by large clusters of adjectives, relative clauses, and reduced relative clauses; (2) the increasing use of nominalizations other than nouns and pronouns for

[6] "The Imitation, Comprehension, and Production of English Syntax —A Developmental Study of the Language Skills of Deprived and Non-Deprived Children," unpublished progress report for Office of Education contract no. 5-10-239, 1968.

[7] *Problems in Oral English*, p. 56.

[8] *Grammatical Structures Written at Three Grade Levels* (Champaign, Ill.: National Council of Teachers of English, 1965).

subjects and objects (clauses and infinitival and gerundive construction, all increasingly unique); and (3) the embedding of sentences to an increasing depth (naturally entailed by (1) and (2)). This elaboration, we note, does not involve correctness. As stated in Chapter Three, elaboration is achieved by embedding or conjoining potentially independent sentences so as to assert several statements in a single, qualified predication within which the statements are logically and subordinately related to each other by syntax. The issue is not that schoolchildren do this incorrectly, although on some attempts they get lost in their own construction; the issue is that they do not do this as much and as often as mature speakers. In other words, they know the transformations requisite for elaboration, and they will elaborate more anyway as they grow up. In asking whether a knowledge of grammar improves writing in this respect, all we are asking is what Piaget calls "the American question": how can we speed it up? But, more fairly stated, we are asking how we can help students to go farther in syntactic growth than they would have otherwise.

The reasons why children do not elaborate as much as adults stem from causes other than ignorance of grammar. Children may forget how they start a sentence construction. They have trouble holding in their minds at once several syntactic relations or levels of embedding. They are not intellectually ready to relate ideas in logical ways other than temporal, or to range ideas in a hierarchy of subordination, or even to perceive the listener's need for such ranging and emphasis. They need to hear and read a lot of elaborated sentences so that they can internalize the forms and relations. And they have to discover, through speaking and writing, the deficiences of simple sentences. They must construct sentences that answer the felt needs of their maturing thought, their exchanges in conversation, and their efforts to fit what they write to what they have to say. There is good reason to believe that the final answer to linguistic elaboration lies beyond language, in general cognitive development, and that intellectual stimulation is far more likely to accelerate syntactic growth than grammar knowledge.

But let's look now at what research has to say about the influence of grammar instruction on composition. If one were to accept the following statement, the whole issue would seem closed.

In view of the widespread agreement of research studies based upon many types of students and teachers, the conclusion can be stated in strong and unqualified terms: the teaching of formal grammar has a negligible or, because it usually displaces some instruction and practice in actual composition, even a harmful effect on the improvement of writing.[9]

But the research studies upon which this statement is based were almost entirely concerned with the goal of error-correction, even when, as in the case of a couple, the data included some counting of sentence constructions in student writing (most of the data in these studies being drawn from objective tests). Nor does the statement include research with transformational grammar, which is only now being put to the pragmatic test. What has been rather definitely proven so far — and this is the exact significance of the quotation above — is that parsing and diagramming of sentences, memorizing the nomenclature and definitions of parts of speech, and otherwise learning the concepts of traditional, classificatory grammar or of structural, slot-and-substitution grammar do not reduce errors. When correctness is the goal, these studies show, an incidental and individual approach to errors is more effective. In other words, the main preoccupation that inspired the bulk of this research — correctness — is precisely that aspect of composition to which grammar study has nothing to contribute.

Only two pieces of research have, as of this writing, attempted to find out (1) if grammar study increases syntactic versatility and (2) if a transformational grammar can succeed where its predecessors have failed. Comparing the writing per-

[9] Richard Braddock, Richard Lloyd-Jones, and Lowell Schoer, *Research in Written Composition* (Champaign, Ill.: National Council of Teachers of English, 1963), pp. 37–38.

formance of 21 students who were taught transformational rules and concepts over a two-year period with the performance of 20 students who were taught no grammar, Bateman and Zidonis[10] concluded that because a generative grammar seems to be a logical representation of the psychological process of sentence formation, a knowledge of such grammar enables students to increase the proportion of well formed sentences they write, to increase complexity without sacrificing grammaticality, and to reduce the occurrence of errors. Two of these conclusions, we note, still concern correctness, but one does make a claim for syntactic elaboration. The assertion about generative grammar being a representation of psychological processes is actually a speculation, not a fact derived from the data, and in fact amounts to a misunderstanding of transformational theory, where no such precise claim is made. No account is given in the report of how the grammar was taught or of the kinds of writing that students were asked to do. But the most serious problem with this research is the methodology, which has been considered very poor and indeed has been used as a bad example in a course on methodology given at Harvard University by an imminent researcher in psychology. Though not reliable in itself, the experiment was a badly needed piece of pioneering, and Bateman and Zidonis are pursuing their investigations.

In the other study, by John Mellon,[11] about 250 seventh-grade students of different schools, socio-economic classes, and academic tracks comprised the population. The experimental group was taught certain transformational concepts and rules of transformation in preparation for the main treatment, which consisted of novel sentence-building exercises that required students to embed one or more dummy kernel sentences into a

[10] Donald Bateman and Frank Zidonis, *The Effect of A Study of Transformational Grammar on the Writing of Ninth and Tenth Graders* (Champaign, Ill.: National Council of Teachers of English, 1966).

[11] *Transformational Sentence-Combining, A Method of Enhancing the Development of Syntactic Fluency in English Composition,* Harvard University, Project 5-8418, Cooperative Research Bureau, U. S. Office of Education.

base sentence according to the previously learned rules. The point of these exercises was to afford students the actual experience of elaborating syntactic constructions they do not normally use, without their being distracted by efforts to make up content or to adapt constructions to rhetorical needs. This treatment was presented as part of a course in language study for its own sake and deliberately divorced from the composition program, so that the a-rhetorical situation considered desirable for the sentence-building exercises would not be misconstrued by students as an adjunct to or substitute for composition. The control group worked its way through one or the other of Warriner's traditional grammar texts, and the placebo group studied no grammar at all. All subjects wrote nine pre-test compositions in various modes of discourse and nine post-test compositions in the same modes. Extensive grammatical analysis — centering on the number and frequency of nominal and relative embeddings, and on clustered modification and depth of embedding — was made of this large corpus of writing. The resulting data made possible not only comparisons of syntactic growth among the three groups but also with the norms for such growth as established by Hunt.

Mellon's study is of great importance. It is the first to establish that some kind of formal language exercises can cause students to write with greater syntactic fluency than normal growth would occasion. The research was intelligently designed, expertly executed, and cautiously interpreted. The experimental group, which had done the transformational sentence-building exercises, was writing at post-test 32% more of the five critical transform types (nominal clauses and phrases, and relative clauses, phrases, and words) than the control group, which had studied traditional grammar. Their rate of growth was more than twice the rate indicated by Hunt's norms. The experimental group ended the year embedding 1.9 secondary statements per independent clause as compared with 1.4 for the control group (a very significant difference when operative over a large amount of writing). In frequency and depth of embedding, and in frequency and size of clustered modification, the experimental group led both control and placebo groups. The fact that the latter two were not significantly distinguishable leads Mellon to conclude:

> First, the growth produced by the sentence-combining treatment represents a significant enhancement of normal growth, regardless of whether the latter is defined in a curriculum environment featuring conventional grammar, or in one with no grammar study of any kind. Second, conventional grammar is in fact a kind of placebo treatment itself, in that the effects which it produces do not differ significantly from those observed in a no-grammar environment. (p. 93)

It is essential to be precise about just what this valuable study proves: *embedding exercises* based on transformational rules will improve syntactic versatility in writing. It does not substantiate the hypothesis that instruction in transformational grammar will produce these results. Mellon states quite explicitly his conviction that what achieved the more-than-normal growth in linguistic elaboration was *the students' experience itself of embedding kernel sentences so as to create complex sentences,* not the learning of transformational nomenclature and rules, which were taught only to facilitate the exercise procedures. In fact, he goes further:

> But turn now to the question of curricular implications which obtain in the findings of this study. It should be remembered first of all that what each of the sentence-combining "problems" actually represents is one mature sentence entered upon the record of the student's total experience in language. Thus the significance of this research, assuming its findings are borne out in future studies covering a wider range of grade levels, pertains only secondarily to the particular format of the sentence-combining activities it investigates, and hardly at all to the model of grammar in the context of whose study they were presented. Rather, its significance resides in its having demonstrated that systematic programs entailing the a-rhetorical, intensive, and specially structured

experiencing of mature sentences, can bring about an increase in the otherwise normal rate at which the sentence structure of the student's own productions becomes more highly differentiated and thus more mature. Subject once again to findings of subsequent studies, it appears further that this increase of growth rate is of sufficient magnitude to justify one's regarding the programs which produce it as valuable supplements to reading, writing, and discussing, which would of course remain the staple activity content of the several subjects in English. (p. 111)

Threading through Mellon's conclusions are two critical matters. The first concerns the rejection of the possibility that learning the concepts and rules of transformational grammar or of any other grammar could improve sentence production. His argument for this rejection is the same I would advance and that seems to enjoy a fair consensus among linguists. To hope, by means of grammatical formulations, to shortcut through the deep, cumulative learning that comes from speaking is to indulge in wishful dreaming. These formulations cannot seriously compete with the profound conditioning of speech habits acquired in the learner's native environment. For children who learned a non-standard grammar at home, description and analysis remain a little body of intellectual knowledge powerless to permeate the automatic process that generates their utterances. To expect such book learning to reverse years of unconscious experience, emmeshed as it is in family and social life, is a ridiculously academic notion. Only because language is symbolic and bound up with ideas would we ever have been so foolish as to entertain this notion. We certainly don't expect other behaviors to be acquired this way. The trouble is precisely that we teachers are prone to conceive language as an external object instead of an internal operation. As for expanding one's linguistic repertory, that certainly must be done by *receiving and producing* sentences oneself. Input indeed is needed: the learner must hear and read many sentence constructions that would not initially come to his mind. But he needs to try out the forms he takes in.

Transformational linguists themselves have never claimed that a knowledge of their grammar will improve a learner's speech or writing. Peter Rosenbaum may be fairly taken as representative:

> The abstract constructs offered in a transformational description are designed solely for purposes of description and explanation. Neither the transformational theory nor the transformational description of the syntax of English contains any implicit pedagogical recommendation. From neither does it follow that a transformational description of English should be taught in the classroom. From neither does it follow that instruction in transformational grammar will improve performance in the literate skills. With respect to the latter assertion, consider an analogy from physical education, in particular the pedagogy of the forward pass. Any instance of the physical event identified as a forward pass has certain mechanical properties which are characterized by the Newtonian theory of mechanics. The descriptive apparatus of this theory, consisting of such constructs as mass, acceleration, velocity, time, distance, and so forth, is a consequence of the theoretical constraints imposed upon a description seeking to account for the mechanics of physical event. To teach a potential quarterback the mechanics of the forward pass is to teach him how this type of event works. It is not to teach him how to make it work. The Newtonian theory itself gives us no reason to believe that instruction in the mechanics of the forward pass will affect the quarterback's becoming a good passer one way or the other. Similarly, to study and practice the constructs of a transformational grammar may result in an understanding of how the student's language works, but not necessarily in an understanding of how to make it work.[12]

The second matter raised in Mellon's research concerns the context in which students underwent the sentence-combining experience that actually accelerated the growth of their written sentences. Teachers must ask not only whether a certain practice achieves the intended effects but whether in doing so it also

[12] "On the Role of Linguistics in the Teaching of English," *Harvard Educational Review,* Vol. 35, no. three (1965), pp. 341–342.

produces undesirable side-effects. In a part of Mellon's research that tested for overall writing quality (outside readers judged an 8% sampling of the compositions) certain possible side effects of the exercises such as the creation of strained, garbled, or torturous sentences were ruled out. But what is not known is whether the a-rhetorical learning context divorced syntactic fluency from syntactic appropriateness, that is, whether the exercises made students value elaboration for its own sake and become facile without relating this facility to those communicative, stylistic, and rhetorical needs that alone make elaboration desirable in the first place. The experimental group did not, according to the readers, produce writing of a higher quality than that of the other two groups, a fact that may be attributable to many other factors besides the experimental treatment and that, indeed, rests on too small a sampling to warrant much concern. It is possible, however, that the learning context in which the sentence-combining tasks took place does enhance facility while neutralizing the compositional judgment that should accompany it.

One reason for thinking that this may be so arises directly out of the very effectiveness with which the sentence-building experience was transferred to writing even though everything was done to keep students from associating it with their work in composition. One purpose of dissociating the exercises from composition was actually to ensure that students did not, when writing, elaborate sentences for no good compositional reasons, as they did essentially of course during the exercises. But if the syntactic skill transferred, why not the "learning set" that surrounded it? The curricular separation of language study from composition cannot ensure that when a student elaborates sentences in his natural writing he does not do so in the same a-rhetorical way he did during the exercises, for the learning and the learning set are bound by a very powerful association. If he learns to coil and embed constructions as an extraneously motivated intellectual feat, he may write his own sentences without regard for the needs of the whole discourse in which they occur and which alone can provide the proper context for them. Not only learning theory but the failure of some sentence exercises of the past give basis to my concern here. For example, students asked to subordinate one of the clauses in a dummy sentence, or to write a modifier-cluster sentence modeled on an example, often get the idea that such constructions are *absolutely* good. At any rate, they will concoct them for no other motive than to comply with what seems to be the teacher's preference, just as they originally subordinated that clause to comply with the exercise directions, instead of doing so because their ideas demanded such a conjunction. I doubt that calling an exercise "language study" rather than "composition" will avert this. It is very dangerous to separate a learning action from the motive that one expects will engender the action in authentic practice. This point in no way undermines the essential validity of the sentence-combining experience; it merely argues for situating the experience within another setting. Mellon himself suggests that the embedding "problems" might be stripped of grammatical appurtenances and made into language-building games for elementary school or incorporated into composition assignments for high school.

Francis Christensen has objected to the Hunt-Mellon measures of syntactic growth on the grounds that these measures may reinforce bad style.[13] One certainly must agree with him that complicated sentences and multiple embeddings can make for awful writing. And who would disagree that much insufferable officialese results from the over-use of long noun phrases? Syntactic complexity is no virtue in itself, surely. But the point is to be *able,* not *obliged,* to complicate one's sentences. Appropriateness — matching language structure to thought structure, and form to effect — must be the criterion. As I suggested, the a-rhetorical nature of Mellon's exercises risks disjoining complexity from appropriateness.

Whether Hunt and Mellon do or do not equate complexity with good style, another part of Christensen's objection seems valid to me, namely that in computing clause length, they have

[13] "The Problem of Defining a Mature Style," English Journal, Vol. 57, no. 4 (April 1968).

failed to discriminate among constructions that have very different effects for style and readability. Thus Hunt and Mellon do seem to imply that long clauses represent maturer writing, whereas, Christensen points out, some of these long clauses contain construction like appositives and absolutes that should not be included in the wordage count of the clause. Christensen argues that, because they make a rhetorical difference, all grammatically "loose or additive or unessential or nonrestrictive" constructions — all "free modifiers" — should be classified separately from the clauses they modify. Accordingly, Christensen claims that the sentences of the best writers will yield, by his analysis, a smaller wordage count per clause. The sort of distinction ignored by the analysis of Hunt and Mellon is illustrated, Christensen says, by the following two sentences:

> The very hallmark of jargon is the long noun phrase — the long noun phrase as subject and the long noun phrase as complement, the two coupled by a minimal verb.

and

> The very hallmark of jargon is the long noun phrase as subject coupled by a minimal verb to the long noun phrase as complement.

The conclusion of Christensen's argument is that the natural growth toward long clauses, especially noun clauses, should not be fostered, as Mellon tried to do, but rather that the twig should be bent. *"Maybe the kids are headed in the wrong direction."*[14] But I think Christensen fails here to allow for the dynamics of language growth. He is assuming that instruction can short-cut development, so that, for example, a student can be deflected from relative clauses to appositives, or from adverbial clauses to absolutes. But children's sentences must grow rank before they can be trimmed. Although I cannot cite evidence to prove this point, I feel certain from studying children's writing that they have to spin out long clauses before they can learn to reduce

[14] Ibid., p. 575.

them. Of the two sentences below I would say that the maturing student has to write the first before he can write the second.

> After he was elected, Goodsayer adopted the policies his opponent was advocating, which he had harshly criticized when he was running for office.

> Once elected, Goodsayer adopted the policies advocated by his opponent — the very policies he had harshly criticized during the campaign.

Three of the four changes are reductions of clauses. Much of the tightness and readability of mature style depends on clause reduction of this sort. And since clause reduction presupposes a prior expansion of clauses, short-cutting is not possible. In other words, I believe the term "clause reduction" refers not only to some sentence transformations but also to a psychological process of language maturation. The pedagogical issue, then, is not whether children's syntax should grow in the direction of more and longer clauses — it must — but, rather, when and by what means students can feel the need for clause reduction and thus learn to exploit it for rhetorical advantage.

Once we bring the notion of clause reduction to bear on problems of sentence complexity, we realize how difficult it is to relate stylistic maturity to any concept of complexity (of which many are being developed today). Intricacy of thought does not necessarily correspond to linguistic intricacy. *That* is merely a demonstrative pronoun whose inclusion in a sentence does not make for snytactic complexity, but if *that* refers to a whole preceding idea, then the sentence may be far more cognitively loaded than its structure would suggest. In this respect, consider some adverbs that act as inter-sentence connectors, such as *however, conversely,* and *in this respect.* And of course it is in the very nature of clause reductions, as we have seen, that length of clauses and sentences should be no true index of stylistic maturity. Indeed, sometimes a single well chosen word can replace an entire clause, producing a far simpler and far better sentence (though any evaluation must depend on a writer's intent). Compare:

I don't like what is left in the cup after you finish drinking.

to

I don't like the dregs.

Unless the speaker wished to convey ignorance of vocabulary itself, the second sentence is better. But the first is considerably more complex. Or should we look at the matter this way: in reducing to a noun a clause-within-a-clause, the word *dregs* is in effect replacing its own definition — *what is left in the cup after you finish drinking.* Therefore the true structure of the simpler sentence includes the nominal clause — the definition of *dregs* that appears explicitly in the more complex sentence but that merely underlies the vocabulary of the simpler one. If syntactic development stands in such close relation to vocabulary development, then one can only regard skeptically any efforts to measure sentence maturity by sentence complexity. Indeed, the argument above casts doubt on the whole effort to evolve a theory of complexity in isolation from semantics and word concepts. Or at any rate a theory so derived seems doomed to superficiality.

Francis Christensen's own work deserves our passing attention because it exemplifies how grammar teaching keeps cropping up under new rubrics, newly rationalized.[15] Christensen's way of analyzing sentences, which has been incorporated into the tenth-grade experimental materials of the Nebraska Curriculum Center, is rather misleadingly called "A Generative Rhetoric of the Sentence." It is generative only in the technical sense of a deductive system, being derived from transformational theory as popularized by Paul Roberts (whose rendition is unacceptable to most transformationalists themselves), not in a psychological sense relating to actual sentence creation. His analysis is indeed rhetorically oriented, since he emphasizes how syntactic differences make a stylistic difference, but students doing his exercises are not placed in a rhetorical situation.

[15] See *Notes Toward a New Rhetoric* (New York: Harper & Row, 1967).

Unfortunately, the yoking of *generative* and *rhetoric* suggests a utility for composition that is not borne out.

Christensen analyzed sentences from well known professional writers and concluded that the good features of their style could be described by four principles — the *addition* to the main clause of clause modifiers, the *direction* of modification (placement of modifiers before or after the clause), the *level of generality* of modifiers in relation to the main clause, and the sentence *texture* that results. The following sample, drawn from his Nebraska unit, and originally written by Irwin Shaw, shows his mode of analysis: the additions are staggered below the main clause, labeled for construction, and numbered for level of generality.

(1) The assistant manager fussed over him,
   (2) wiping a cut on his leg with alcohol and iodine, (VC)
      (3) the little stings making him realize how fresh and whole and solid his body felt. (AB)

This differs from purely grammatical analysis in only one important respect: the numbering of abstraction levels, which brings in a semantic factor, does indicate that the writer states the broadest generality in the main clause, which he places first, and states the details in ensuing clause modifiers of descending abstraction level. Christensen claims that this kind and direction of modification characterizes the great majority of narrative and descriptive sentences in contemporary professional writing. Consequently he has devised two sorts of classroom exercises that embody this analysis. In one, the student brackets and numbers the various modifying constructions in sample sentences such as the one above, and in the other he combines two or three dummy sentences so as to "restore" a particular sentence as originally written. Clearly, the first is old-fashioned grammar parsing with a slightly new twist, whereas the second closely resembles Mellon's sentence-combining exercises, even to the stipulating of which structure is to result from the combining. Furthermore, Christensen's exercises presuppose a course in formal grammar. In other words, the Nebraska unit on "generative rhetoric" is vulnerable, on the one hand, to the same old criticism leveled at any other kind of grammatical analysis — that no evidence justifies it as a teaching procedure for composition. After all, grammar-composition approaches have always tried to relate syntactic differences to effective style; there is nothing new here in method. On the other hand, the unit prompts the same objection as to Mellon's exercises — that combining dummy sentences outside the real writing situation divorces syntax from judgment.

At first glance, Christensen may seem to have precluded such a separation since, in contrast with Mellon's a-rhetorical approach, Christensen has *told* the students that they are doing the exercises to provide them with good structures for narrative and descriptive writing. But pre-teaching rhetorical rules of good style, as I will argue at length in the following chapter, does not help students evolve an effective rhetoric, whether the rules derive from Aristotle or from a study of the best contemporary writing. By distilling a formula from the sentences of professionals Christensen has made the descending clause-modification structure a doctrinaire kind of absolute good, whereas it should always remain one option among others, its relative virtues to be ascertained by trial comparison with these other options. The very criterion of appropriateness that Christensen invokes against Hunt and Mellon becomes jeopardized in his own exercises. The assigning of abstraction levels to clause modifiers, which is his real contribution, serves better to describe what writers do than to prescribe what novice writers should do. If it is true that professionals characteristically construct their sentences deductively, opening with a main clause that sets the general scene or action first and afterwards adding details in clause modifiers, then it is reasonable to assume that such a widespread tendency answers a correspondingly widespread need in readers to see the whole tableau before proceeding to its parts. Such matters are historically and culturally relative, however. Much haiku poetry, for example, not to mention some passages in Faulkner, move inductively from the unsituated detail to the frame of reference. In these cases the writer deliberately does not orient the reader until after the reader has tried to orient himself. It is precisely as a *psychological* matter of orientation that analysis by levels of abstraction becomes rhetorically significant.

The "direction of modification" does indeed make a difference in effect since it indicates a whole-to-part or part-to-whole orientation. But, first of all, the teacher should not himself prefer one or the other on the grounds that one characterizes the writing of his own epoch. In this respect, secondly, one feels that Christensen over-reacts to the outmoded canon of style that preferred the periodic sentence. He is right to point out that contemporary writers do not follow the old principle "Shift the modifier to the head of the sentence," but he is replacing one dogma with another. The fault is to *prescribe* anything. Third, whatever the orientation, a writer may wish to subordinate the most general statement into a modifier and raise the detail into the main clause: "As he was fussing over him, the manager wiped the cut on his leg with . . . ." (See the original Shaw sentence on page 175.) Thus a deductive sentence orientation plus a certain logic of subordination will *require* that the modifier precede the main clause. Only a comparison of sentence alternatives — in the context of what the writer is trying to accomplish — will teach judgment. Finally, a sequence of images may ascend or descend in generality not only throughout a single sentence but throughout a series of sentences, paragraphs, or stanzas as well. Which is to say that the opportunity to learn consists precisely of deciding *whether* to combine the sentences of the exercise or to leave them as they are, whether to parcel out the image sequence over a string of Christensen's "additions" or over a string of independent sentences or even larger units. Without options, and the reasons for options, it is futile to speak of teaching rhetoric. And the options must be made apparent during the composing process, not settled in advance by a dictum of good style.

In sum, the activity of combining sentences undoubtedly constitutes a powerful teacher of syntax — if related to will and choice, and if will and choice are exercised during authentic discursive tasks. What Mellon and Christensen try to do by arraying sentence types in sequential exercises can be better done, I submit, by exploiting the sentence-combining activities ordinarily entailed in naturalistic tasks. Although embedding-transformations cannot in this way be precisely sequenced, the trading of systematization for organic learning may prove a wise bargain.

Any sort of revision can entail appropriate sentence-combining if the revision process is well directed. In Chapter Three I tried to demonstrate how the revision process of discussion becomes internalized and thus causes the individual to incorporate sentences into each other. The necessary condition here is that the dialogue be a collaborative development of a subject, and this usually requires some discussion training. Other sorts of revision are proposed in *A Student-Centered Language Arts Curriculum*. One sort occurs in a pure game situation when one child makes up a short sentence, passes it to a partner to expand in any way that occurs to him, takes the sentence back to expand further, and so on, the object being to make together the longest sentence they can.[16] Another sort occurs when students rewrite sensory or memory notes into a composition.[17] For the sake of economy, one often notes ongoing sensations and memories in a clipped, staccato fashion, producing sentence fragments or kernel sentences that need to be combined when composing from these notes later. A class discussion of sample notes can indicate some of the sentence-combining possibilities before students cluster in small groups to read each other's notes and make similar suggestions. It is during the preparatory class discussion that the teacher's knowledge of sentence analysis can come into play.

More generally, any composition revision, whether based on notes or not, can include sentence-combining (or clause reduction). Let me illustrate. Suppose that students have written a piece of narrative, reportage, or fiction. The teacher projects or dittos one of the incoming papers and leads a discussion de-

[16] See page 155, *A Student-Centered Language Arts Curriculum*.
[17] *Ibid.*, Chapters 9, 13, and 14.

signed to help students make suggestions to each other for revision when they break into small groups afterwards. Let's say that one student has written:

> The assistant manager fussed over him and wiped a cut on his leg with alcohol and iodine. The little stings made him realize suddenly how fresh and whole and solid his body felt.

By any number of means, the teacher can suggest that students consider other structures for this sentence sequence. The class may express some difficulty in understanding the passage or some concern about the style, in which case the teacher invites suggestions for revision. Or the teacher may simply change some sentences, in the spirit of tinkering, and ask for reactions to different versions:

> Fussing over him, the assistant manager . . . .
> The assistant manager, fussing over him, wiped . . . .
> As the assistant manager was fussing over him, wiping a
>   cut . . . , the little stings made him . . . .

What difference do these changes in emphasis and effect make, in the opinion of the class? Would other rewritings be better? Should the sentences remain as they were? The teacher or a student might propose as a possibility the exact sentence that Irwin Shaw wrote, but maybe that would not be the best sentence for this piece of writing. What does the student author think? Which revision would he accept? Does the class agree, knowing now his intention? Then the teacher proposes that they suggest and discuss similar sentence revisions for their papers in small groups. By this means the concepts of Christensen and the transformationalists may influence student writing, not narrowly and systematically but constantly and organically. Sentence-embedding and clause reduction can occur in mid-composition as two of several options, another of which is to break one sentence down into smaller ones.

Some complete discourses are one sentence long — certain poems, including some haiku, and such things as maxims, proverbs, and epigrams. Only when the sentence unit defines the form should the unit of study be the sentence. If students write these discourses, exchange them, and tinker with them, in a spirit of creative play, they can learn an enormous amount about significant syntactic possibilities.[18]

Following out now the earlier notion that cognitive stimulation may be the best developer of syntax — especially of *appropriate* syntax, let me give two examples from some trials of sensory writing. While watching some third-graders write down their observations of candle flames — deliberately this time, not merely in note form — I noticed that sentences beginning with *if-* and *when-* clauses were appearing frequently on their papers. Since such a construction is not common in third-grade writing, I became curious and then realized that these introductory subordinate clauses resulted directly from the children's *manipulation of what they were observing*. Thus: "If I place a glass over the candle, the flame goes out." And: "When you throw alum on the candle, the flame turns blue." Here we have a fine instance of a physical operation being reflected in a cognitive operation and hence in a linguistic structure. Consider also the following nominal clause, taken from a sixth-grade class where the pupils were dropping liquids of varying viscosity from varying heights onto papers of varying absorbency: "The drops it makes are almost indestructible." This embedding of one kernel sentence into another (*It makes drops. The drops are almost indestructible.*) resulted directly and organically, I feel, from the pupil's effort to render exactly what he saw, to specify *which* drops are indestructible, *it* referring obviously to one of the three liquids and his task being to discriminate among the three by testing for differences. Similarly, the cognitive task entailed in the candle tests *created a need* for subordinate clauses, because the pupils were not asked merely to describe a static object but to describe changes in the object brought about by changing conditions (*if* and *when*).

In summary, there are alternative methods to grammar teaching for developing syntactic maturity. Sentence-expansion

[18] For work with one-sentence discourse, see *pp.* 361 and 463, *A Student-Centered Language Arts Curriculum.*

games, good discussion, rewriting of notes, collaborative revision of compositions, playing with one-sentence discourses, and verbalizing certain cognitive tasks are the alternatives I would recommend. The cognitive tasks build sentence structure along the referential dimension of discourse while revision from feedback builds sentences along the rhetorical dimension. Transformational theory has rendered a service by inspiring people such as Mellon and Christensen to devise sentence-combining tasks, but since transformational theory itself merely reflects syntactic options confronting people when they discourse, sentence-combining may operate powerfully throughout the curriculum without referring to the theory that describes it and without confining it to the small context required by research.

Unfortunately, transformational theory has also inspired a wholly different rationale for teaching grammar than the old one about improving speech and writing, which for many educators and linguists stands discredited on both empirical and logical grounds. The new case is that teaching some form of transformational concepts is an essential part of a humanistic education. In the same article quoted earlier, Peter Rosenbaum makes the case for this school of thought.

> In providing the most general account of linguistic structure, the transformational approach to linguistic inquiry yields new insights into human intellectual capacity, namely, those innate properties of the human mind which allow for the acquisition and use of language. In pursuing this capacity through the linguistic mechanisms which underlie competence in language, the student is involving himself in a study which has had intrinsic intellectual appeal for centuries, the study of those abilities which make human beings human.[19]

At first this may have a plausible ring, perhaps because it insists on the word "human," but it is a specious argument, I'm afraid — one that I'll have to take issue with. The mere fact

[19] "On the Role of Linguistics in the Teaching of English," pp. 343–344.

that it is of a human subject does not make a description a humanity, especially if that description derives from mathematical and symbolic logic. The mode and abstraction level of the description are critical. Transformational grammarians are committed to describing linguistic *competence* — that is, the ideal capacity that some generalized speaker of a language seems by inference to possess. To use their distinction, competence is quite different from *performance,* which includes all the actualities and accidents of real situations — speaker-temperament, audience influence, ongoing circumstances, etc., which accompany any authentic instance of speech. In short, all those palpable, particular, familiar, *human* qualities are missing (no fault for research perhaps, but a serious fault for school learning). What makes history, literature, conventional philosophy, and a lot of material in the behavioral sciences humanistic is that either they treat particular instances of things relatable to one's own behavior and observation (this relating being already a considerable feat of abstraction), or else they generalize directly from such instances. If someone were to describe lovemaking by charting relations of heartbeat, electrical potential, skin temperature, and brain waves (possibly a very useful description for some purposes) I would not therefore classify this description as humanistic, however dear the activity may be to human practitioners.

A severe limitation of both older and new linguistics is that they deal with no structure larger than the sentence. Such circumscribing of the field of inquiry is of course what defines a discipline, but to impose on the English curriculum, as a humanity, a discipline that does not rise above the level of syntax is hardly rational. The power and import of language become apparent only when we go well beyond the processing of phonemic and morphemic sequences into well formed sentences — not only to chains of sentences and paragraphs but to large verbal behaviors within and among people. What is humanistic is precisely what lies beyond the bounds of linguistics, which is a drastically small context for studying man's symbol-making capacity. More appropriate are those individual and group arenas that psychology and sociology have staked out. It would be extremely difficult to maintain that linguistics should enjoy the status of a required subject, as part of English, when those other disciplines having a much clearer claim to the status of humanities — and which, in fact, are fast incorporating linguistics — are generally not taught at all before college.

That transformational theory applied as a research tool in psychology, sociology, and anthropology will in the future yield insights that should legitimately appear in the school curriculum — yes, that I can certainly accept as a possibility. Indeed the quick adoption of transformational theory for analytical purposes by important researchers in other disciplines, as by psycholinguists Roger Brown and David McNeil, testifies to its value. But educational benefits will be necessarily indirect for school study of how the mind works. It is understandable that university researchers working in the brilliantly advancing discipline of linguistics should hold hopes for a great yield of knowledge and want that knowledge to be taught in school. But to recommend that their research theories be in some way incarnated as a content in the English curriculum betrays both the misguided zeal of a junior science feeling its oats and the insensitivity of the university theoretician to the learning process of pre-college students. The following statement is tell-tale: "The educational implementation of a transformational description of the structure of English introduces the student to the live tradition of scholarship and language study. . . ."[20]

Now that we are barely beginning to exorcise the grammar ghost, I would hate very much to see it conjured from another quarter, certified by the prestige of some of our finest thinkers and licensing a notorious weakness of many schools, which can now feel free to play the old grammar game but with new texts and a clear conscience.

Other rationales have been advanced for grammar teaching, old and weak but persistent. One hears, for example, "Shouldn't

[20] *Ibid.*, p. 344. From the fact that Rosenbaum has recently put out school textbooks it is clear that by "implementation" he means direct substantive teaching of transformational grammar.

grammar be taught as an aid to learning foreign languages?" But a decision to teach grammar for this reason amounts to taking sides in an important controversy among foreign language teachers, many of whom abhor the grammar–translation method and espouse a more "direct" method based on conversation and oral pattern drills. At any rate, if foreign language teachers want students to know formal grammar, let them teach it. "But a knowledge of grammatical terms helps the teacher discuss composition with his students." If a teacher feels such a need for the vocabulary for parts of speech, kinds of clauses, and types of construction — *adverb, subordinate,* and *appositive,* for example — then let him set aside a class period to name and illustrate these things, supplying a couple of handout sheets for reference. Merely learning the nomenclature does not require a course, a textbook, etc. We hear still another voice, however: "Grammar disciplines the mind — it teaches students to think logically." The answer to this is that ordinary language is far too ambiguous for training in formal logic. Instead let's offer a course in symbolic logic itself and not fool around with an inferior system.

The latest rationale for a grammatical focus, however, deserves serious consideration because, though unwisely formulated so far (mostly because of a linguistics bias), it speaks in principle to an important educational goal. The term that seems to be emerging for this goal is "rational inquiry." The argument goes like this: Students should become involved in the basic process of examining data and ascertaining facts, in the creation of knowledge through generalization from instances. But, continues the argument, what corpus of data is so familiar to students that they can conduct an honest inquiry into it? Language itself constitutes such a corpus. Any student has produced and received enough speech to be an expert. So let us propose certain inquiries to students and let them find the answers. For example: "What do all sentences have in common?" The class examines lots of sentences and distills for an answer something like a subject and a predication about that subject. Then they may test this out by examining other sentences until they run afoul of imperatives. Are these exceptions?[21] Or, more narrowly: "What kind of things do we say can be frightened (What class of nouns can be objects of *to frighten*)?[22] Such inquiry can be conducted without textbooks, though teachers may need help in asking good questions and in directing the inquiry.

While endorsing enthuiastically the main point of this proposal, I see several problems, all stemming from the unnecessary limitation of inquiry to the realm, once again, of the sentence. First, there are facts about language that students know and facts they don't know. Since they can manipulate syntax orthodoxly it seems reasonable to assume that they know, intuitively, the grammatical fact they are being asked to "discover." The question, then, is what value there is in formulating explicitly something they already know intuitively. The real purpose of inquiry, after all, is to find out something one doesn't know. Second, unless situated in a larger context, questions about the sentence will seem arbitrary and academic to most students. What is the motivation for *grammatical* inquiry? Third, inquiry restricted to syntax will, I'm afraid, blend only too easily into the phony "discovery" approach so widely advertised today, wherein some small facts are programmed for "induction." That is, the students are not "told the facts" in the old fashioned way; they are told the facts in a new fashioned way, the improvement being in the *subtlety* of the manipulation. This is certainly not the intent and spirit of those proposing rational inquiry into language, but my point is that by circumscribing inquiry to syntax they risk subverting unwittingly and unnecessarily their own noble goal. The difference between real and phony discovery depends on whether the teacher can predict what stu-

[21] Wayne O'Neil, "The Misuses of Linguistics in the Classroom: Paul Roberts' Rules of Order," *The Urban Review,* summer, 1968 (Center for Urban Education, 33 W. 42nd St., New York, 10036). This article is a devastating criticism, on both pedagogical and linguistic grounds, of the *Paul Roberts English Series* (New York: Harcourt, Brace & World, 1966). Professor O'Neil is a transformational linguist.

[22] This example is taken from a forthcoming article by Samuel Jay Keyser of Brandeis University.

dents will discover and when. And the difference between trivial and significant inquiry depends on the initial size of the arena.

As with sentence-combining exercises, my recommendation is to leave the sentence within its broader discursive context. Students should raise questions about language to which they truly want to find answers. These will no doubt often lead down to the sentence. Suppose, for example, that they ask, "Why do people communicate through language instead of through other means?" At first, such a question seems hopelessly general, but it is precisely the job of inquirers to sharpen and subdivide questions until the questions become answerable, and answerable by some clear means. In determining what language can do that other media cannot, students may well ask eventually, as a subquestion of their main inquiry, "What do all statements, or sentences, have in common?" In this way, the examination of syntax can, because of its context, yield truly new insight that students honestly want (their original question being prompted, let's say, by the current concern that visual media may supplant language). Similarly, if students generate a question about the difference between the language of poetry and that of prose, they could quite logically end up examining the classes of nouns that can be the objects of certain verbs: normally only animate things can be frightened, but in poetry the thunder may frighten the house.

Rational inquiry into language must not be allowed at its very outset to fall prey, like composition, to the overblown influence of sentence analysis. It is quite clear, if one thinks about it, that grammar tyrannizes over language teaching not because the sentence unit is a sensible learning unit but because we think we know more about the sentence than about whole pieces of discourse, which cannot be analysed with nearly the same precision. But our inability to get a convenient intellectual handle on discourse above the sentence level does not mean that we should adjust education to fit the severe limitations of research instruments. If we teach only what we "know" in this limited technical sense, then we are committing a colossal cop-out.

Ignorance becomes an excuse for further ignorance. Actually, since we practice the various discourses every day, we certainly know them in whatever way we need to know them to help the next generation practice them. Furthermore, sentence definition is not so neat, nor discourse definition so obscure, as appears at first blush. Both are determined by a speaker's decisions about where to begin and end, decisions that depend ultimately on personal choice as conditioned by all the various performance factors.

Point of view is critical here. Seen as a *fait accompli*, as a specimen pinned to the board, a given sentence looks deceptively discrete and self-contained, but if teachers have anything to learn from transformational theory, it is this: any such given sentence *might have been* embedded as a clause or reduced clause in a more complex sentence, or *might have been* strung into a sequence of several sentences. It is only from the point of view of the finished utterance that one can even speak of a sentence. From the viewpoint of language *production,* there are only options about how to parcel out thought into syntax. No grammar can tell us how people play these options, for the reasons are psychological and social, not linguistic. And it is these reasons the teacher must help students to relate to the linguistic forms. He can do so only if the units of learning are units larger than the hindsight sentence. But no reasonable unit exists — surely no arbitrary sequence of sentences or paragraphs — until one reaches that unit which is determined by some speaker's decision to open his figurative mouth somewhere and to close it somewhere else. It's about time the sentence was put in its place.

CHAPTER SIX

Learning to Write by Writing

Most of what I have had to say so far has concerned curriculum. In this chapter my concern is method, in particular the sort of method most appropriate for the notion of curriculum that has been expounded.

What is the main way in which human beings learn to do things with their minds and bodies? Let's not think first about learning to write — we'll get to that soon enough. Let's think about learning to walk, ride a bicycle, play a piano, throw a ball. Practice? Coaching by other people? Yes, but why does practice work? How do we become more adept merely by trying again and again? And what does a good coach do that helps our trials get nearer and nearer the mark? The answer, I believe, is feedback and response.

Feedback

Feedback is any information a learner receives as a result of his trial. This information usually comes from his own perception of what he has done: the bicycle falls over, the notes are rushed, the ball goes over the head of the receiver, and so on. The learner heeds this information and adjusts his next trial accordingly, and often unconsciously. But suppose the learner cannot perceive what he is doing — does not, for example, hear that the notes are rushed — or perceives that he has fallen short of his goal but does not know what adjustment to make in his action. This is where the coach comes in. He is someone who observes the learner's actions and the results, and points out what the learner cannot see for himself. He is a human source of feedback who supplements the feedback from inanimate things.

But, you may say, learning to write is different from learning to ride a bicycle or even learning to play the piano, which are, after all, physical activities. Writers manipulate symbols, not objects. And they are acting on the minds of other people, not on matter. Yes, indeed. But these differences do not make learning to write an exception to the general process of learning through feedback. Rather, they indicate that in learning to use language the only kind of feedback available to us is human response.

Let's take first the case of learning to talk, which is a social activity and the base for writing. The effects of what we do cannot be known to us unless our listener responds. He may do so in a number of ways — by carrying out our directions, answering our questions, laughing, looking bored or horrified, asking for more details, arguing, and so on. Every listener becomes a kind of coach. But of course a conversation, once launched, becomes a two-way interaction in which each party is both learner and source of feedback.

Through their research in the early stages of language acquisition, Roger Brown and Ursula Bellugi have been able to

Except for slight alterations, the text of this chapter was delivered as a lecture on April 7, 1967, at the Yale Conference on English and printed in the *Papers of the Yale Conference on English,* copyright © 1967 by the Office of Teacher Training, Yale University. Reprinted by permission of Edward Gordon, Director of the Conference.

identify two clear interactions that take place between mother and child.[1] One is the child's efforts to reproduce in his own condensed form the sentence he hears his mother utter. The other is the mother's efforts to expand and correct the child's telegraphic and therefore ambiguous sentences. Each time the mother fills out his sentence, the child learns a little more about syntax and inflections, and when the child responds to her expansion of his utterance, she learns whether her interpretation of his words was correct or not. Linguists never cease to marvel at how children learn, before they enter school, and without any explanations or teaching of rules, how to generate novel and well-formed sentences according to a paradigm or model they have unconsciously inferred for themselves. In fact, many of the mistakes children make — like *bringed* for *brought* — are errors of overgeneralization. This ability to infer a generality from many particular instances of a thing, which also accounts for some children's learning to read and spell even without phonics training, is of course itself a critical part of human learning. The learner's abstractive apparatus reduces a corpus of information, such as other people's sentences, to a usable rule. It is a data-processing gift that enables us to learn *something*, but not how to *do* something.

To learn to talk, the child must put his data into action and find out what happens. Thus he learns his *ir*regular verbs when he says, "I bringed my cup," and some adult replies, "Well, I'm glad you brought it." Throughout school, imitation of others' speech, as heard and read, remains a major way of learning language forms, but conversational response is the chief means the child has for making progress in speech production itself. Later, after the syntax and inflections have become pretty well fixed, the responses the learner gets to what he says are not expansions but expatiations. That is, his listener reacts to his ideas and his tone, picks up his remarks and does something further with them, so that together they create some continuity of subject.

[1] Reported in "Three Processes in the Child's Acquisition of Syntax," *Language and Learning*, Janet Emig, James Fleming, and Helen Popps, eds. (New York: Harcourt, Brace, and World, 1966).

Learning to use language, then, requires the particular feedback of human response, because it is to other people that we direct speech. The fact that one writes by oneself does not at all diminish the need for response, since one writes for others. Even when one purports to be writing for oneself — for pure self-expression, if there is such a thing — one cannot escape the ultimately social implications inherent in any use of language. As George Herbert Mead argued so well, even in our unuttered thoughts, we speak as though to another because we have long since incorporated the otherness of the social world to which language is irrevocably tied. Furthermore, we have all had the experience of looking back on something we have written earlier and of responding much as another person might do. Thus, once beyond the moment of writing, the writer himself becomes "other," and can feed back helpfully to himself.

But no feedback of whatever sort can help the learner if his will is not behind his actions, for will is the motor that drives the whole process. Without it, we ignore the results of what we have done and make no effort to adjust our actions so as to home in on the target. The desire to get certain effects on an audience is what motivates the use of speech. This is what rhetoric is all about. So the first reason why one might fail to learn is not caring, lack of motivation to scan the results and transfer that experience to the next trial. The other principal cause of failure is, on the other hand, a lack of response in the audience. One cares, one makes an effort, and no one reacts. For me, the character Jerry, in Albee's *The Zoo Story* epitomizes the desperation of one who cannot get a response. To get some effect on the unresponsive Peter, he runs through the whole rhetorical gamut — chitchat, anecdotes, questions, shocking revelations, quarreling, until finally he resorts to tickling, pushing, and fighting. It is Jerry who says, "We *must* know the consequences of our actions." And sarcastically: "Don't react, Peter, just listen."

Speaking from his experience with autistic children who had withdrawn and given up, Bruno Bettelheim has touched on the importance of both initiation and response. From the very first, he says, an infant should be given the chance to communicate his needs, not have them anticipated, and be responded to when he is communicating the need, not fed according to some other timing.

> It is for this reason that time-clock feedings are so potentially destructive, not merely because they mechanize the feeding, but because they rob the infant of the conviction that it was his own wail that resulted in filling his stomach when his own hunger timed it. By the same token, if his earliest signals, his cry or his smile, bring no results, that discourages him from trying to refine his efforts at communicating his needs. In time he loses the impulse to develop those mental and emotional structures through which we deal with the environment. He is discouraged from forming a personality.

But those are infants, not adolescents, and we teach our students to write, we don't feed them. Bettelheim continues:

> Even among adults the joke that fails to amuse, the loving gesture that goes unanswered, is a most painful experience. And if we consistently, and from an early age, fail to get the appropriate response to our expression of emotions, we stop communicating and eventually lose interest in the world.

"But," we say, "I praise my students, I give them an encouraging response."

> But this is not all. If the child's hungry cry met with only deep sympathy and not also with food, the results would be as bad as if there had been no emotional response. . . . should his smile, inviting to play, be met with a tender smile from the parent but lead to no playing, then, too, he loses interest in both his environment and the wish to communicate feeling.[2]

Smiling, gushing, or patting the back are not to the point. A response must be real and pertinent to the action, not a standard, "professional" reaction. Any unvarying response, positive or not, teaches us nothing about the effects of what we have done.

---

[2] These quotations are from "Where Self Begins," *The New York Times Magazine*, February 17, 1966. The article itself was drawn from *The Empty Fortress*, by Bruno Bettelheim (New York: Free Press of Glencoe, Inc., 1967).

If, as I believe, writing is learned in the same basic way other activities are learned — by doing and by heeding what happens — then it is possible to describe ideal teaching practices in this way and compare them with some current practices. Ideally, a student would write because he was intent on saying something for real reasons of his own and because he wanted to get certain effects on a definite audience. He would write only authentic kinds of discourse such as exist outside of school. A maximum amount of feedback would be provided him in the form of audience response. That is, his writing would be read and discussed by this audience, who would also be the coaches. This response would be candid and specific. Adjustments in language, form, and content would come as the writer's response to his audience's response. Thus instruction would always be individual, relevant, and timely. These are precisely the virtues of feedback learning that account for its great success.

Clearly, the *quality* of feedback is the key. Who is this audience to be, and how can it provide a response informed enough to coach in all the necessary ways? How is it possible for every member of a class of thirty to get an adequate amount of response? Classmates are a natural audience. Young people are most interested in writing for their peers. Many teachers besides myself have discovered that students write much better when they write for each other. Although adolescents are quite capable of writing on occasion for a larger and more remote audience and should be allowed to do so, it is difficult except in unusual situations to arrange for this response to be relayed back to the writers. For the teacher to act as audience is a very intricate matter fraught with hazards that need special attention.

First, although younger children often want to write to a "significant adult," on whom they are willing to be frankly dependent, adolescents almost always find the teacher entirely *too* significant. He is at once parental substitute, civic authority, and the wielder of marks. Any one of these roles would be potent enough to distort the writer-audience relationship; all together, they cause the student to misuse the feedback in ways that severely limit his learning to write. He may, for example, write what he thinks the teacher wants, or what he thinks the teacher doesn't want. Or he writes briefly and grudgingly, withholding the better part of himself. He throws the teacher a bone to pacify him, knowing full well that his theme does not at all represent what he can do. This is of course not universally true, and students may react in irrelevant and symbolic ways to each other as well as to the teacher. But in general, classmates are a more effective audience.

The issue I want to make clear, in any case, is that the significance of the responder influences the writer enormously. This is in the nature of rhetoric itself. But if the real intent of the writing is extraneous to the writing — on a completely different plane, as when a student turns in a bland bit of trivia to show his indifference to adult demands — then the effect is actually to dissociate writing from real intent and to pervert the rhetorical process into a weird irony. Much depends of course on the manner of the teacher, and, curiously enough, if the teacher shifts authority to the peer group, which is where it lies anyway for adolescents, and takes on an indirect role, then his feedback carries a greater weight.

But, it may be argued, students are not informed and experienced enough about writing to coach each other. Won't their feedback often be misleading? How does the teacher give them the benefit of his knowledge and judgement? Let's look a moment at just what students can and cannot do for each other. Part of what they can do is a matter of numbers; multiple responses to a piece of writing make feedback more impersonal and easier to heed. Group reactions establish a consensus about some objective aspects of the writing and identify, through disagreement, those aspects that involve individual value judgments. It is much easier for peers than for the teacher to be candid and thus to give an authentic response, because the teacher, usually aware of his special significance, is afraid of wounding his students. A student responds and comments to a peer more in his own terms, whereas the teacher is more likely to focus too soon on technique. A student, moreover, may write off the comments of a teacher by saying to himself, "Adults just can't understand," or "English teachers are nit-pickers anyway," but when his fellow human beings misread him, he has to accommodate the feedback. By habitually responding and coaching, students get insights about their own writing. They become much more involved both in writing and in reading what others have written.

Many of the comments that teachers write on themes can be made by practically any other person than the author and don't require a specialist. The failure to allow for the needs of the audience, for example, is responsible for many difficulties indicated by marginal comments like, "misleading punctuation," "unclear", "doesn't follow", "so what's your point?", "why didn't you say this before?", and so on. Irrelevance, unnecessary repetition, confusing organization, omitted leads and transitions, anticlimactic endings, are among the many things that anyone might point out. Again, numbers make it very likely that such things will not only be mentioned if they are problems, but that the idiosyncrasy of readers will be cancelled out. Probably the majority of communication problems are caused by egocentricity, the writer's assumption that the reader thinks and feels as he does, has had the same experience, and hears in his head, when he is reading, the same voice the writer does when he is writing. It is not so much knowledge as awareness that he needs.

What help can a teacher give that peers cannot? Quite a lot, but the only time he makes a unique contribution to the problem of egocentricity is when the students all share a point of view, value judgement, or line of thought that they take for granted, in which case one may question whether the teacher can or should try to shake their position, which is probably a factor of their stage of growth. Imposing taste, standards, and attitudes that are foreign to them is futile and only teaches them how to become sycophants. But there is value in the teacher's expressing his point of view so they at least know that theirs is not universal.

Where the teacher can be most help, however, is in clarifying problems after students have encountered or raised them. Adolescents — or, as I have discovered from experimenting, even fourth-graders — can spot writing problems very well, but often they do not have enough understanding of the cause of a problem to know how to solve it. This insufficient understanding more than anything else causes them to pick at each other's papers in a faultfinding spirit or to make shallow suggestions for change. A student reader may complain, for example, that a certain paper is monotonous in places and suggest that some repeated words be eliminated. But the real reason for the monotony, and for the repeating of the words, is that there are too many simple sentences, some of which should be joined. The teacher projects the paper with the comment about monotony and leads a problem-solving discussion. This is where the teacher's knowledge, say, of a generative grammar comes in — not as technical information for the students but as an aid to the teacher. Embedding some of the sentences in others involves, as well as transformations, the issue of subordination and emphasis, so that the problem of monotony can now be seen as also a lack of focus.

The teacher, in other words, helps students to interpret their initially vague responses and to translate them into the technical features of the paper that gave rise to them. Notice the direction of the process — the emotional reaction first, then the translation into technique. This amounts to sharpening response while keeping it paramount, and will help reading as well as writing. While helping to solve specific writing problems, the teacher is at the same time dispelling the negativism of comments and creating a climate of informed collaboration in which feedback is welcomed.

The role of the teacher, then, is to teach the students to teach each other. This also makes possible a lot more writing and a lot more response to the writing than a teacher could otherwise sponsor. He creates cross-teaching by setting up two kinds of group processes — one that he leads with the whole class, and a smaller one that runs itself. It is in the first kind, which I just illustrated, that the judgment and knowledge of the teacher are put into play. Periodically, the teacher projects papers for class discussion, without presenting them as good or bad examples and without trying to grind some academic ax. No detailed preparation is needed. He picks papers embodying issues he thinks concern students and need clarifying, getting his cues by circulating among the small groups, where he learns which problems are not getting informed feedback. He asks for responses to the projected paper and plays these responses by alert questioning designed to help students relate their reactions to specific features of the paper before them. If they indicate problems, he asks them to suggest changes the author might make. In these class discussions the teacher establishes tone and a method of giving and using feedback that is carried off into the small groups.

The procedure I recommend is to break the class into groups of four or five and to direct the students to exchange papers within their group, read them, write comments on them, and discuss them. This would be a customary procedure, run autonomously but constantly reinforced by the model of class discussion the teacher continues to lead. It can be of help *during* the writing process, before the final draft. The small size of the group, the reciprocity, tend to make the comments responsible and helpful. The teacher makes it clear that all reactions of any sort are of value — from strong emotions to proof-reading. A writer should know when he has succeeded in something; honest praise is very important. Descriptive remarks are very helpful — of what the paper seems to be or do, and of the effects it had on the reader. All these responses can be compared by talking over together the comments on each paper. Later in this discussion, the author says what he meant to do, and suggestions for bringing the paper more in line with his intentions are made if needed. The teacher sits in on the groups in rotation, acting as consultant and joining the discussion without necessarily having read the papers.

After the sessions, the papers may be revised. The more use to which they are put, the better. In fact, the small groups would most of the time act as editorial boards to prepare papers for some purpose. Themes should be printed up, exchanged with other groups just for reading, performed, and many other

,hings. Eventually they go into folders kept for each student and when the teacher has to evaluate student work for the benefit of administration, he makes a general assessment of the writing to date. No grades are given on individual papers.

The teacher of course may respond individually to any paper at any time during a discussion or during a conference. Whether he writes comments on the paper himself depends on several things. Do his students still need an adult to validate and give importance to their work? In his commentary helping or hindering? Is it necessary? If a student does not want a certain paper read by anyone but the teacher (which happens less often in small groups, where trust is stronger), the teacher honors the request and serves as reader and commentator himself. For some assignments the teacher may feel that his comments are especially relevant, for others not. In any case, if student cross-commentary occurs during the writing process and is at all effective, the amount of commentary the teacher needs to make should be small, as indeed it should be anyway. Mainly, the teacher has to know the effects of *his* action, how students are taking his feedback. First-person comments are best and will set an example for student cross-commentary. A teacher should react as an audience, supplementing the peer audience. Above all, a piece of writing should not go to a dead-letter office. Both the non-response or the irrelevant response persuade the learner that nothing is to be gained from *that* line of endeavor, and the impulse to write withers.

Trial and Error

I would like now to go back to aspects of the action-response model of learning other than the quality of the feedback. These have only been implied so far. Plunging into an act, then heeding the results, is a process of trial and error. That is the first implication. Now, trial and error sounds to many people like a haphazard, time-consuming business, a random behavior of children, animals, and others who don't know any better. (Of course, by "random" we usually mean that we the observers are ignorant of the reasons for the behavior.) Trial and error is by definition never aimless, but without help the individual alone may not think of all the kinds of trials that are possible, or may not always see how to learn the most from his errors. And if it is a social activity he is learning, like writing, then human interaction is in any case indispensable. So we have teachers to propose meaningful trials (assignments) in a meaningful order, and to arrange for a feedback that insures the maximum exploitation of error.

The second implication is that the teacher does not try to prevent the learner from making errors. He does not preteach the problems and solutions (and of course by "errors" I mean failures of vision, judgment, and technique, not mere mechanics). The learner simply plunges into the assignment, uses all his resources, makes errors where he must, and heeds the feedback. In this action–response learning, errors are valuable; they are the essential learning instrument. They are not despised or penalized. Inevitably, the child who is afraid to make mistakes is a retarded learner, no matter what the activity in question.

In contrast to the exploitation of error is the avoidance of error. The latter works like this: the good and bad ways of carrying out the assignment are arrayed in advance, are pretaught, then the learner does the assignment, attempting to keep the good and bad ways in mind as he works. Next, the teacher evaluates the work according to the criteria that were laid out before the assignment was done. Even if a system of rewards and punishments is not invoked, the learner feels that errors are enemies, not friends. I think any learning psychologist would agree that avoiding error is an inferior learning strategy to capitalizing on error. The difference is between looking over your shoulder and looking where you are going. Nobody who intends to learn to do something wants to make mistakes. In that sense, avoidance of error is assumed in the motivation itself. But if he is allowed to make mistakes with no other penalty than the failure to achieve his goal, then he knows why they are to be avoided and wants to find out how to correct them. Errors take on a different meaning, they define what is good. Otherwise the learner engages with the authority and not with the intrinsic issues. It is consequences, not injunctions, that teach. We all know that, don't we?

But doesn't this process lead to more failures? A learner needs very much to feel successful, to score. If he learns everything the hard way, doesn't he get discouraged by his mistakes? For one thing, trial-and-error makes for more success in the long run because it is accurate, specific, individual, and timely. For another, if the teacher in some way sequences the trials so that learning is transferred from one to the next, the student writer accumulates a more effective guiding experience than if one tried to guide him by preteaching. And feedback of the sort I am advocating — because it is plentiful and informed — does not just leave a feeling of failure, of having "learned the hard way," in the sense of coming out a loser. When response is real and personal, it does not leave us empty, even if our efforts missed their mark.

The procedure, moreover, of getting feedback *during* the writing instead of only *afterwards* allows the learner to incorporate it into his final product (as, incidentally, adults do when we are writing professional articles). I recommend also a lot of chain-reaction assignments, such that one paper is adapted into another. This amounts to a lot of rewriting, not mere tidying up but taking a whole new tack under the influence of suggestions from other students. It is with the isolated, sink-or-swim assignment that the student goes for broke. Finally, the error-avoiding approach has hardly given students a feeling of confidence and success; since it is the predominant method of teaching writing, it seems fair to attribute to it a lot of the wariness and sense of failure so widespread among student writers today.

The Case Against Textbooks

The third implication of action–response learning follows from the last one about the futility of preteaching writing problems. If we learn to write best by doing it and by heeding the feedback, then of what use is the presentation of materials to the learner? Don't presentations violate the trial-and-error process? Don't they inevitably entail preteaching and error-avoidance? My answer is yes. If I reject all prepared materials for writing, it is not that I am failing to discriminate among them. I know that they come in all sizes, shapes, and philosophies. It is not the quality but the fact of these materials that I am speaking to.

The assumption I infer from textbooks is that the output of writing must be preceded and accompanied by pedagogical input. Now, there are indeed some kinds of input that are prerequisites to writing — namely, conversation and reading — but these are very different from the presentations of textbooks. Let's look at the sorts of materials that are used to teach writing.

This material may be classified into six overlapping sorts, all of which might appear in any one unit or chapter. The first sort consists of advice, exhortation, and injunction. It is the how-to-do-it part, the cookbook material. Here are some fabricated but typical samples. "Make sure you allow for your audience." "Catch the reader's interest in the first sentence." "Make sure your punctuation guides the reader instead of misleading him." "Connect your ideas with linking words that make transitions." "Write a brief outline of the points you want to make, then write a paragraph about each point." "For the sake of a varied style, it is advisable to begin some sentences with a main clause and others with subordinate clauses or phrases." "A vivid metaphor will often convey an idea more forcefully than a lengthy, abstract explanation." "Build up your descriptions from details that make your readers see." "A good narrative has a focus or point to it that is not obscured by irrelevant details (remember what we learned about focus in the last unit?)."

What is wrong with practical pointers and helpful hints? As I have suggested, preteaching the problems of writing causes students to adopt the strategy of error-avoidance, the teacher's intention clearly being to keep them from making mistakes.

The learner is put in the situation of trying to understand and keep in mind all this advice when he should be thinking about the needs of the subject. The textbook writer is in the position of having to predict the mistakes that some mythical average student might make. The result is that, in true bureaucratic fashion, the text generates a secondary set of problems beyond those that an individual learner might truly have to deal with in the assignment itself. That is, he has to figure out first of all what the advice means at a time when it can't mean very much. Often he makes mistakes because he misconstrues the advice. In trying to stick to what he was told, he is in fact working on two tasks at once — the fulfillment of the advice and the fulfillment of the assignment.

Since not all learners are prone to the same mistakes, some of the pointers are a waste of time for the individual personally; he would not have erred in those particular ways. The exhortations and injunctions often inhibit thought. But most critically of all, they prevent both the learner and his responders from knowing what he would have done without this preteaching. It is essential to find this out. The learner has to know his own mind, what it natively produces, so that he can see what he personally needs to correct for. Students who fulfill the advice well have passed the test in following directions but have missed the chance to learn the most important thing of all — what their blind spots are.

After all, allowing for the audience, catching interest in the first sentence or paragraph, guiding the reader with punctuation, making transitions, varying the style, using metaphors, giving narrative a point — these are common-sense things. What interests me is why a student fails to do these things in the first place. The fact is, I believe, that writing mistakes are not made in ignorance of common-sense requirements; they are made for other reasons that advice cannot prevent. Usually, the student *thinks* he has made a logical transition or a narrative point, which means, again, he is deceived by his egocentricity. What he needs is not rules but awareness. Or if he omits stylistic variation, metaphor, and detail, he does so for a variety of reasons the teacher has to understand before he can be of use. Scanty reading background, an undeveloped eye or ear, a lingering immaturity about not elaborating are learning problems that exhortation cannot solve. Particular instances of failing to do what one thinks one is doing, and of failing to use the full resources of language, should be brought to light, the consequences revealed, the reasons explored, the need for remedies felt, and the possibilities of solution discovered. Unsolicited advice is unheeded advice, and, like time-clock feeding, imposes the breast before there is hunger.

A second class of material found in textbooks is expository. Here we have the definitions and explanations of rhetoric, grammar, logic, and semantics. In other words, information about language and how it is used. Part of the game played here is, to borrow the title of a Henry Read poem, the naming of parts. The assumption seems to be the primitive one that naming things is mastering them. It goes with the attempt to convert internal processes into an external subject. By pedagogical slight of hand, an output activity is transformed into something to be read about. The various ways of constructing sentences, paragraphs, and compositions are logically classified and arrayed. The student can then be put to work on writing as if it were any other substantive content: he can memorize the nomenclature and classifications, answer questions on them, take tests, and on some fitting occasion, "apply" this knowledge.

The explanations tell him what it is he is doing when he strings utterances — not he, of course, but some capitalized He, for this is the realm of general description and theory. The material may be up to date — the new linguistics and the new rhetoric — but the method couldn't be older: "There are three kinds of sentences: simple, complex, and compound." "Articles, demonstratives, and genitives make up the regular determiners." "An inductive paragraph goes from particulars to the main statement, and a deductive paragraph begins with the main statement and descends to particulars." "Ideas may be presented in any of several patterns: they may be repeated, contrasted, piled up in a series, balanced symmetrically, and so on." The elements of fiction are plot, character, setting, and theme." "People use the same words, but don't mean the same things by them."

Such generalities, like advice, induce in the students a strategy of avoiding errors, of trying to do what the book says instead of doing justice to the subject. Whereas advice tells you what you *should* do with language, exposition tells you what people *do* do; it codifies the regularities of practice. The message is essentially the same: apply these rules and you will be all right. Good teaching, rather, helps the individual see what he in particular is doing with language and, by means of this awareness, see what he in particular might be doing. There is no evidence that preteaching general facts and theories about how people use language will help a student learn to write. (The teaching of grammar as an aid to composition is such a special and notorious case in point that I dealt with it separately in the last chapter.)

Since the most natural assumption should be that one learns to write by writing, the burden of proof is on those who advocate an indirect method, by which I mean presenting codifications about rhetoric and composition in the hope that students will apply them. Today there are many good theories of rhetoric and composition. Teachers should study these, for, like grammatical formulations, they may help the teachers understand what their students are doing or not doing in their writing. But to teach such formulations, through either exposition or exercises, would hinder more than help.

A third class of materials comprising textbooks is exercises. Sometimes the student is asked to read some dummy sentences and paragraphs and to do something with them. For example: "Underline the one of the following words that best describes the tone of the sentence below." "Rewrite the sentence that appears below so that one of the ideas is subordinated to the other." "Change the order of the sentences in the following paragraph so that the main point and the secondary points are better presented." "Read this paragraph and underline the one of the sentences following it that would serve as the best topic sentence." "Make a single sentence out of the following." Or the student may be asked to make up sentences or paragraphs of his own: "Write a sentence describing some object or action, using modifier clusters as in the examples." "Write a descriptive paragraph following a space order (or a time order)."

Exercises are obviously part and parcel of the preteaching approach characterized by advice and exposition. A point raised and explained in the text is simply cast into the form of directions so that the student will apply the point directly. The philosophy here is a curious blend of hard-headed logical analysis and folklorish softheadedness. That is, the teaching of "basics" is construed in this way. Basics are components, particles — words, sentences, and paragraphs. The learner should manipulate each of these writing units separately in a situation controlling for one problem at a time. He works his way from little particle to big particle until he arrives at whole compositions resembling those done in the outside world. The single-unit, single-problem focus derives from linguistic and rhetorical analysis done in universities, not from perceptions about learning.

The folklorish part is represented in the old saw about having to crawl before you can walk. But crawling is an authentic form of locomotion in its own right, not merely a component or sub-skill of walking. For the learner, basics are not the small-focus technical things but broad things like meaning and motivation, purpose and point, which are precisely what are missing from exercises. An exercise, by my definition, is any piece of writing practiced only in schools — that is, an assignment that stipulates arbitrary limits that leave the writer with no real relationships between him and a subject and an audience. I would not ask a student to write anything other than an authentic discourse, because the learning process proceeds from intent and content down to the contemplation of technical points, not the other way.

First of all, when it is the stipulation of the text or the teacher and not the natural limit of an utterance, a sentence or a paragraph is too small a focus for learning. How can you teach style, rhetoric, logic, and organization in a unit stripped of those authentic relationships to subject and audience that *govern* the decisions about word choice, sentence structure, paragraph structure, and total continuity? Judgment and decision-making are the heart of composition. With exercises the learner has no basis for choosing one word or sentence structure over another, and rhetoric becomes an irony once again. It is a crime to make students think that words, sentences, paragraphs, are "building blocks" like bricks that have independent existence and can be learned and manipulated separately pending the occasion when something is to be constructed out of them.

And when students make up a sentence or paragraph demonstrating such and such kind of structure, they are not learning what the teacher thinks they are: they are learning that there is such a thing as writing sentences and paragraphs for their own sake, that discourse need not be motivated or directed at anyone, that it is good to write even if you have nothing to say and no one to say it to just so long as what you put down illustrates a linguistic codification. The psychological phenomenon involved here — called "learning sets" by H. E. Harlow, and "deutero-learning" by Gregory Bateson[3] — is that when someone learns a certain content, he also *learns that way of learning*. This second kind of learning tends to be hidden because it is not under focus, and yet for that very reason may be the more lasting. The student learns how to do exercises, and this learning is of a higher order, ironically, than the learning of the different sentence or paragraph structures contained in the exercises. Thus in an a-rhetorical learning situation, he learns to discourse a-rhetorically!

When decomposition precedes composition, many such unintended and harmful side-effects occur that seem to go on unnoticed because we are fastened on the logic of the subject instead of the psychologic of the learner. Scientists have long been aware that when you isolate out a component for focused observation, you are changing it. Live tissue under a microscope is not live tissue in the body. A sentence or paragraph stripped

[3] See pp. 215 and 216 of *Communication: The Social Matrix of Psychiatry,* by Jurgen Ruesch and Gregory Bateson (New York: W. W. Norton & Company, Inc., 1951).

of its organic context, raised several powers, and presented in the special context of analysis and advice represents serious tampering with the compositional process, the consequences of which are not well recognized.

Second, a student doing a paragraph exercise, say, knows the problem concerns paragraph structure, whereas in authentic discourse the real problem always is this, that *we don't know what it is we don't know.* A student may do all of the exercises correctly and still write very badly because he is used to having problems plucked out of the subjective morass and served to him externally on a platter, and has consequently developed little in the way of awareness and judgment. For example, he *can't* decide how to break into paragraphs because he must write only one paragraph.

Third, students adopt a strategy for beating the game of exercises: they take a simplistic approach, avoid thinking subtly or complexly, and say only what can lend itself readily to the purpose of the exercise. To make the paragraph come out right, they write things they know are stupid and boring.

Fourth, the poetic justice in this strategy is that the exercises themselves ignore the motivational and learning needs of the student. The result is just the opposite intended: the learner dissociates the technical issues in the exercise from honest discourse. The learner becomes alienated, not only by this but by the hidden message of exercises, which says, "We are not interested in what you have to say; we just want a certain form." His defense is to do the exercise by the book in an ironically obedient fashion to show them for just what they are. You bore me and I'll bore you. This dissociation in the minds of students between school stuff and writing for real is one of the deep and widespread symptoms that has made English teaching ripe for reform.

The last three kinds of materials are not bad in themselves but suffer from being embedded in the paraphernalia I have been polemicizing about. For this reason I will deal with them briefly. The first is the presentation of samples of good writing to serve as models. As I have said, learning to write entails a lot of reading, but when passages from the old pros are surrounded by rhetorical analysis and pesky questions about how Saroyan got his effects, a disservice is done to both reading and writing. How would you as an adolescent react to a message such as this: "See how Steinbeck uses details; now you go do that too." And there is no evidence that analyzing how some famous writer admirably dispatched a problem will help a student recognize and solve his writing problems. From my own experience and that of teachers I have researched with, I would say, rather, that models don't help writing and merely intimidate some students by implying a kind of competition in which they are bound to lose. The assumption is still that advance diagnosis and prescription facilitate learning. The same reading selections could be helpful, however, if merely interwoven with the writing assignments as part of the regular reading program but without trying to score points from them. Learners, like the professional writers themselves, incorporate anyway the structures of what they read; what they need is more time to read and write authentically. The service publishers could do is to put out more straight anthologies of whole reading selections grouped according to the various kinds of writing but unsurrounded by questions and analysis. The student should write in the forms he reads while he is reading them. There can be a lot of discussion of these selections, but the points of departure for discussion should be student response to the reading.

Another kind of textbook material — writing stimulants — is closely related to models because sometimes these prompters are also reading selections. Or they may merely be the text writer's own prose as he tried to set up ideas or talk up topics, two intentions that are better realized in class conversation. Sometimes the stimulants are photographs — possibly a good idea, but the pictures are always too small in the textbook. Whatever the kind of stimulant, the wiser course is to let it arise out of the daily drama of the student's life in and out of school, including his regular reading. In this way the stimulants are automatically geared to what the students know and care about. To present stimulants in a book is to run an unnecessary risk of irrelevance and canned writing.

At last we come to the assignment directions themselves. They, of course, are justified, but for them who needs a book? Even the windiest text writer could not get a textbook out of assignment directions alone. It is better anyway for the teacher to give the assignment because he can adapt it to his particular class — cast it in a way that they will understand, relate it to their other work, and so on.

Let me summarize now my concerns about presenting materials to students as a way to teach writing. They install in the classroom a mistaken and unwarranted method of learning. They take time, money, and energy that should be spent on authentic writing, reading, and speaking. They get between the teacher and his students, making it difficult for the teacher to understand what they need, and to play a role that would give them the full benefit of group process. They add secondary problems of their own making. They sometimes promote actual mislearning. They kill spontaneity and the sense of adventure for both teacher and students. They make writing appear strange and technical so that students dissociate it from familiar language behavior that should support it. Their dullness and arbitrariness alienate students from writing. Because they predict and pre-package, they are bound to be inappropriate for some school populations, partly irrelevant to individual students, and ill-timed for all.

I believe the teacher should be given a lot of help for the very difficult job of teaching writing. A lot of what is in textbooks should be in books for teachers, and is in fact partly there to educate them, not the students. The real problem, as I think many educators would admit, is that too many teachers cannot do without textbooks because they were never taught in schools of education to teach without them. Textbooks constitute a kind of inservice training in teaching method and in linguistic and rhetorical analysis that they never received before. Thus the trial-and-error approach would be considered too difficult for most teachers; they wouldn't have the background, perception, and agility to make it work. The extreme of this belief is that teacher-proof materials are necessary to compensate for teacher inadequacy. If this is so, then let's be frank and solve the problem by renovating teacher training and by publishing more books for teachers on the job, not by putting materials in the hands of students. If it is acknowledged that textbooks do not exist because they embody the best learning process but because teachers are dependent on them, then we would expect them to dwindle away as the education of teachers improves. But I don't see that texts are a mere stop-gap measure. There is every indication that they will become more powerful, not less. The investments of everyone are too great. I don't mean just the publishers, who are merely supplying a demand; I mean that we are all caught in a self-perpetuating cycle that revolves among education schools, classrooms, school administrations, and publishers. The teaching of writing will not improve until the cycle is broken. It is not up to the publishers to break it; they will put out whatever teachers call for. Although a number of teachers do teach writing without texts, it is too much to expect a revolution to start in classrooms without a lot of change in school administration and schools of education, which is where the cycle can be broken.

If I have strayed here into essentially noneducational considerations, it is because I believe the only justification for textbooks in writing is an essentially noneducational one. My main purpose has been to propose that writing be taught naturalistically, by writing, and that the only texts be the student productions themselves. I regret that I have had to speak so long against something, but it is not enough to propose; a way must be cleared. I see tremendous evidence against the preteaching approach, embodied in textbooks, and no evidence for it. The great advances in language theory, on the one hand, and in programming techniques on the other, are unfortunately reinforcing that approach. The prospect that frightens me is that we educators are learning to do better and better some things that should not be done at all. We are rapidly perfecting error. Which is to say that I think we should heed better the feedback we get about the consequences of our own teaching actions.

If most of the ideas entertained in this book have merit, one far-reaching conclusion must be drawn from them: the division of learning into English, Mathematics, Science, and Social Studies is a huge mistake. The reason I have insisted on the term "discourse" is to show that what we usually call "English" cannot be successfully conceived as merely a separate subject in an array of other subjects.

Because one discourses in his native language about *all* matters and at many abstraction levels, there is really only one subject (aside from art, music, and physical education), and that subject is discourse itself, of which science and social studies are subclasses. The latter are correctly viewed either as bodies of content (symbolized) or as ways of processing information (symbolizing). As content, they are what one discourses about; as process, they are acts of discoursing. Either way they are not subjects separate from and coordinate with the native language, but specialized examples of the functioning of that language. Mathematics, on the other hand, being a symbol system itself, is an extension of ordinary discourse into special notation, the value of which is to gain concision and economy and to reduce the cognitive load of thinking. Mathematical symbols can be spoken and read and can be transliterated back into that ordinary language from which they derive (though admittedly with some loss of meaning in the case of very advanced mathematics). In short, I have not been talking in this book just about "English teaching" but, inevitably, about a whole curriculum, though, again inevitably, in a tentative way.

So I would like to end with the proposal that educators work toward a future reorganization of the total curriculum that would eliminate conventional subject divisions and would base learning on the central process of human symbolization. The distinctions between modes and levels of abstraction are far more important than distinctions in subject content. The most important things children of today will need to know when they are adults are how experience is abstracted, communicated, and utilized, whether the data are recurring phenomena of nature and society or the private truths of the heart.

Information and definitions accumulated from the past — about geography, peoples, machines, nature — all require the same basic reception and treatment by the learner, namely, the will to know, decoding and comprehension, and the assimilation of knowledge into one's prior knowledge systems. These are not specialties of any one subject, and student failures in these subjects are notoriously traceable to such general discursive problems. Furthermore, the teaching of both the social and natural sciences has recently taken a turn toward process, emphasizing less the accumulation of facts than the ways in which natural and social scientists go about ascertaining facts. These ways are basic abstractive methods that should be practiced by learners all through school; they are not unique to one field or subject and should not appear so to students upon the abrupt introduction of a certain "course."

Correspondingly, mathematics teaching has taken a turn toward the understanding of logical principles and away from the memorization of procedures. But the separation of mathematics from English and the empirical subjects breaks the essential continuity between the specialized notation of mathematics and ordinary language, and between the semantic power of mathematics and the data upon which this power can be brought to bear. Mathematical story problems, for example — how many gallons of water flow through a half-inch tap in two hours — require just this ability I am implying to move with ease back and forth between everyday speech and the special notation of mathematics. Beyond this, the failure of many youngsters in mathematics stems simply from poor motivation because the "problems" are pointless exercises, not real problems that arise in the context of, say, learning about mechanics. One symptom of this separation is the great difficulty schools have in coordinating mathematics instruction so that a learner will have studied such-and-such kind of equation in time to do so-and-so sort of physics problem.

But poor coordination is only one effect of our fragmented, ill-conceived curriculum. Waste, inefficiency, and inconsistency are appalling. Basic processes like group discussion, sensory recording, textual comprehension, data gathering, inference making, and verbal composition are critical for virtually all subjects, but none of these receives adequate attention and some are treated only incidentally if at all. The reason for this dereliction is that a given process is considered the province of one subject — as when logic is placed under geometry, "reading comprehension" under English, sensory observation under science — so that no one process gets continuous and comprehensive treatment at all ages. Makeshift efforts may be made, of course, to "get a little logic into the English course" or "work on reading comprehension" in science, but all these efforts show is that none of these things are being taught well anywhere and that integration is desperately needed. Learning the native language entails virtually all the problems encountered in any other subject, and yet there is neither the time nor the means to teach for these problems in an isolated English course (especially when the course is filled with thoughtless rituals). The remaining subjects, on the other hand, also continue to be badly taught, despite current reforms, because the basic abstractive processes upon which they depend fall neither into their bailiwick, except briefly by default, nor into the bailiwick of "English." The current organization of the curriculum features inessentials of content difference and slights the essentials of human symbolization.

What a fundamentally reorganized curriculum would look like I do not know, though I have tried in Chapter Two to suggest the beginnings of a model. Many of our best minds will have to work on this problem in the next few years. Certainly the old "core curriculum" or the joint teaching of *The Grapes of Wrath* by a litterateur and a Gov.-Ec. man do not touch the heart of the matter, though such endeavors do represent some sort of felt need, however inadequately conceived. I should think, however, that reorganization would center on the learner as producer and manipulator of symbols. If he is adept at abstracting and at understanding the abstractions of other people, this learner will have no trouble acquiring the accumulated knowledge of the past, which in any case he will have to select according to a future we do not know and which will certainly revise considerably whatever we might select for him. Content coverage, in short, simply cannot be allowed to remain the educational issue it has been. Actually, in playing the range of the discursive spectrum, in some such way as I have tried to envision in *A Student-Centered Language Arts Curriculum, Grades K-13,* the learner will become well acquainted with literary, scientific, and utilitarian sub-discourses, *in relation to each other,* and necessarily cover a lot of content anyway even though this content is not segregated into subjects.

Nothing less than the growth of the whole human being requires a new integration of learning. What is common to all subjects should be the unifying force of schools, and what is common is precisely the human capacity to symbolize first- and secondhand experience into an inner world to match against and deal with the outer world. The infant does this already. Such a capacity is not taught; it can only be exercised more or less beneficially. It operates integratively on all fronts at once, at all ages. Education as we know it hinders the growth of this capacity perhaps more than it fosters it. The learner expends most of his intelligence coping with the demands of arbitrary contents and arbitrary schedules instead of using his native apparatus to build his own knowledge structures from what he and others have abstracted. Since the latter is what he will spend the rest of his life doing, whatever the future, this primary activity, I submit, should gain priority over all else in education.